Mind Your Business

6 Key Strategies Guaranteed to Help You Speak and Live Your Truth

By Juanita P. Guerra, Ph.D.

DEDICATION

I humbly dedicate this book to Mami. I am who I am because of everything you poured into me. Te amo con todo mi corazón hoy y siempre!!! Bendición.

I dedicate this book to my brothers as well. Though things were not perfect between us, there was absolute perfection in our process. I love you all forever and a day!

ACKNOWLEDGEMENTS

More than anyone else I would like to thank my friend, my spiritual advisor, my editor, Stephanie Quarles. You walked this journey with me from beginning to end. You read the book before the book and helped me to understand the importance of telling my story and using what I have learned to help others. I can't thank you enough.

Lauren Hunter, Madelyn Ortiz, Claire Moreno, Gregory Newman and Joel Fridovich thank you all for your willingness to read my story and give me the necessary feedback to make it better. I am eternally grateful to each of you.

A special thank you to Gina Marie Franzel. Your unending support, laughter, and encouragement made a difference.

Last, but not least, my unending gratitude goes to Susan Hart. First you bowed down, then you tore me up, then you said "Wow." You organized my writing and pushed me to be brave and make a difference. You have an immensely generous spirit and loving heart. It is my honor to call you my friend.

Contents

Introduction

My Desire for Us All: A Formula for Success

As a psychologist, for years, I dreamed of finding a formula for success that could help everyone walk in their greatness. At first, the formula for success I envisioned was complicated and had many moving pieces. Then, the idea of writing this book came to me. Initially, I thought this book would be about my life story and my triumphs. Then, I realized I could use my story to break down this complicated formula for success into a set of key strategies that can help people live their lives in a manner that is as genuine as possible. While there is no specific magic formula to end all human suffering, the formula for happiness and success boiled down to something as simple (but not easy) as developing a set of strategic mechanisms to help individuals live in their authenticity.

I am no expert on God or the Bible. However, I have unwavering faith in God and believe that God wants us all to honor our true selves, and to use our individual gifts and talents to serve others. I also believe that God's plan is for all of us to be fruitful and successful. This plan is not something that is just for a select few. God's plan is available to everyone who is willing to do something as simple, yet difficult as live their truth. Two old sayings apply here: "To thine own self be true" and "The truth shall set you free." My life and work experiences have taught me that a disconnect from our true selves and a God of our understanding are the primary reasons many people are unhappy. For me, the definition of success is being genuine to myself. Success is being able to fulfill your purpose and use your God-given gifts to serve humanity. Simply stated, success is being intentional in your actions, honoring your greatness, and being yourself!

It is my hope that sharing my experiences and what I have learned will help others live their lives in a manner that is as authentic as possible.

Part I – My Family Experiences

A Little About Me

When I was an adolescent, I loved to read The National Enquirer, a tabloid newspaper with celebrity drama and hard-to-believe stories. I was nosy and drawn to others' tales and life drama from a very young age. Looking back, it makes complete sense that I went on to become a clinical psychologist, dedicating my life's work to focusing on real-life dramas. I love listening to people tell me their stories. They fascinate me and intrigue me. People's experiences are unique and challenging, and no two are alike.

We all have a story to tell and can learn from one another's experiences if we listen with open minds and open hearts. That's what I do for a living. I sit, and I listen to individuals share their intimate narratives with a compassionate ear. As they tell me their stories, I never fail to experience a sense of gratitude that they chose me to share their vulnerability with, and I honor this gift by being the best therapist I can be to them. If it isn't yet obvious, please know that I love what I do for a living.

I trained to be a psychodynamic, insight-oriented clinician, but there is nothing formal or traditional in how I practice psychotherapy. At the beginning of my career, I was more conventional in engaging the individuals I counseled. However, time and experience have shown me that the more formal and traditional therapeutic approaches don't always work for everyone. I gradually developed clinical skills that spoke more genuinely to who I am as a person.

Time and experience have taught me that a disconnect from our core sense of self and the great I AM (the Creator of all that is) is at the core of most human suffering. I know that speaking and writing my truth may set me up to be ridiculed or judged. It may also alienate some people. The mere mention of a Divine Being often makes people uncomfortable because they think you're going to start preaching or pushing your beliefs onto them. That is not what I am here to do. Instead, I want to make clear from the beginning both the immense power of my faith in a God of my understanding, and my belief that feeling disconnected from this Almighty Source is the core reason for a lot of unnecessary human suffering.

I'm at a point in my life where I feel grounded, strong, and brave enough to take a leap of faith and share some of my experiences and the lessons I have learned from them. I hope that sharing some of these things, along with some of my ideas of what I believe and feel, may make it easier for others to share their stories. I have unbelievable faith in the power of healing through sharing and processing our experiences together. Let me say that again, I believe in the power of healing through sharing and processing our experiences together. Telling our stories helps us feel less alone and allows us to learn from one another.

As I thought about sharing some of my experiences, I realized that it might be even more helpful to share some of the strategies I have learned over time that have helped me live more genuinely and connect to my core self. These techniques allow me to be as authentic as possible at any given moment. I believe in these strategies so much that I use them as the foundational base to guide my work with others. Admittedly, none of these strategies are brand new. You will see that they are all familiar. The key to them being helpful resides in utilizing them intentionally and consistently in your efforts to live your life as the Almighty Creator intended you to. That is, to live your truth and fulfill your purpose.

My Family Now

I am a single mother to "three children:" two amazing teenagers and my mom. All three drive me crazy, and yet I love them more than anything else in life. My home has recently become a dorm. The COVID-19 pandemic has us all home, on a pause of sorts, redefining our lives in these unprecedented times. The kids are online, playing video games, listening to music, on their phones, sleeping, and cooking at all hours. Mami, my mom, and I cook, eat, tell stories, and laugh throughout the day. What else is there to do during a pandemic? We are fortunate! In these trying times, our home life feels light-hearted and serene for the most part. We have our occasional ugly blowouts, but then we reset, and life goes on.

I am not only a daughter and a mom, but I am also a sister to three older brothers that drive me crazy! There are just no words for their idiosyncratic behaviors (sigh). To fully understand and appreciate my perception of life and my strategies, you first need to meet and understand my mom, brothers, and family. Sharing with you some of the experiences that led to the development of crazy, wonderful Me will help put into context how those experiences impacted how I perceive the world and how I interact with people.

My Family Then

I am proudly a product of my environment. That pride comes from the reality that while reared in chaos, I overcame the hurdles that were a part of my everyday environment. I grew up in a poor, drug-infested, Hispanic and Black neighborhood in the Boogie Down Bronx. My single, Puerto Rican mother raised four children with limited finances and no significant support system. It sounds like a recipe for disaster, right? It sure was, at first. We were a mess for a very long time. But out of this madness eventually evolved four amazing, intriguing adults with inspiring lives and stories of their own. I am going to share my version of our story. My perception. My experiences. My truth. I hope that one day my brothers will share their stories too.

Where do I start...

The Beginning of My Story

To grasp the depth of my story, you have to understand the world I come from and all its complexities. I am the youngest of four children, born to a traditional Puerto Rican woman. My mom has an old-school, classic, Latina mentality. She proudly cares for her home and her family, regardless of the impact it has on her. In other words, she believes that the better she cares for her home and family, the more valuable she is as a woman. From an early age, Mami pushed me also to be a classic Latina. She expected me to embrace domesticity and to accept the traditional female role of our culture. The expectation was for me to also love and care for my family in a martyr-like manner, as only a woman could. However, taking on and accepting this traditional role did not come naturally to me. Mami and I both knew it, but neither of us wanted to accept it. I wanted nothing to do with cooking, cleaning, or anything domestic in nature. This truth caused a lot of tension between us. Mami did not understand why I struggled to follow this cultural expectation. She often told me, "I don't understand the kind of woman you are growing into." She couldn't understand or accept the real me as I was growing up.

Since early childhood, I preferred to engage my mind in things that made me think. I didn't fit into my mother's preconceived notions of what a daughter and a female should be. Like every child, I wanted my mother's approval. I desperately wanted to be loved and accepted by Mami. When I was very young, I tried to be what she expected and wanted me to be, but because it wasn't who I was naturally, at my core, I did not do a great job. Sadly, even then, I knew that Mami didn't accept me for who I was and that she was disappointed in me. You could see it in her facial expressions, in her exasperation with me when I did something that was not up to par with her expectations. Mami strongly delivered, very early in my life, the message that I was somehow not good enough as I was, as I AM.

Mami

To understand my family dynamics, you have to understand each of us individually. Let me back up and start at the top with Mami. Mami was reared in a family where she was verbally, emotionally, and psychologically abused. Her family life was so hostile and toxic that she left home at 16 and never returned. With only an eighth-grade education, Mami had no significant support system and struggled to provide for herself. Eventually, she met an older man whom she hoped would love and care for her, but he was an alcoholic who mistreated her. Moreover, he had a wife and a family when he met Mami, and he never left them. Mami was naive and vulnerable, so she remained in this adulterous relationship and had my two oldest brothers with this man. He was abusive towards Mami, even physically assaulting her while she was pregnant with her second child. To her credit, once he struck her, Mami immediately ended this relationship. She was brave to walk away from her abuser, penniless, with a toddler and another child on the way.

Sadly, Mami's subsequent two relationships also ended badly. Both my third brother's father and my father were also addicts and abusive towards Mami. Eventually, Mami ended up on her own with four children to raise, no significant family support system, and limited finances. Mami struggled to care and provide for herself and her children. She made a lot of mistakes, but ultimately did the best that she could.

Because Mami had a rough life, she, like many in her shoes, struggled with anxiety and depression. I remember Mami was often quiet in her room, always anxious and worried that she would not be able to pay the bills or feed us. She often looked sad and was always exhausted. Although sometimes she was playful and loving, most often, she just seemed frustrated and angry. It must have been difficult for Mami to navigate all of her emotions and experiences while trying to care for her children. All of these hardships adversely impacted us individually and collectively. While I can't speak for my brothers, I felt bad for Mami even as a child. She was alone and lonely. I felt guilty and sad that I could not diminish her pain and suffering and could not help her more.

5

Mami was like the walking wounded. She was hurting in her heart and soul, but life's demands dictated that Mami compartmentalize her inner turmoil and focus on basic survival and the care and well-being of her children. To her credit, no matter what she was struggling with or how she felt, she always remained focused on her primary goals of keeping us fed and providing us a home. Survival was the name of the game; everything else was secondary. Mami worked in a factory and relied on government assistance to provide the basics for herself and her children. She lived in a perpetual state of being overwhelmed. The struggle was real for Mami. Mami had minimal support from her family and no real guidance on living life in an empowered manner.

What kept Mami from unraveling? What guided her, and how did she keep her head above water? Mami was not a religious person. She didn't go to church or do things outwardly that spoke to her belief in God. Mami nevertheless believed with her heart and soul in God, and her faith in God is what kept her afloat. Her faith never wavered. No matter what happened, good or bad, Mami always told us, "Everything happens for a reason," "God knows what he's doing," and "You have to have faith in God." She strongly believed that as long as she had faith in God, she was never alone, and things would work themselves out in her favor. Mami's core faith in God is the best example of the expression "Walk by faith, not by sight," and is probably the most important thing she taught me.

Mami and I had a complicated experience; she was at the core of my challenges with understanding and accepting who I was at a soul level. Yet, she also provided me with the essential tools I needed to survive, thrive, and live in my essence. Mami is a complex and enlightened being, and I am grateful for all that I have learned from her.

While my relationship with Mami was ultimately rich and life-altering, I felt lost and confused by my experiences with her for a long time. I was too young and immature to comprehend the many layers of our relationship: parent-child, only daughter, the youngest child, cultural expectations, etc., and that she was doing the best she could with what she had. In my youth, I could not appreciate the complexity of our interactions.

My experiences with my brothers were similar, but not as intense or dramatic, mainly because my mother mattered more to me than they did. To understand my brothers, you have to know some of their backgrounds as well.

My Brothers and Our Three Fathers

My two oldest brothers have the same father, but they each had a very different relationship with him. My first brother was very close to his father and is also very much like him in personality. He is entertaining, charismatic, funny, and engaging, but he can also be selfish, self-absorbed, and sexist. His presence can be intoxicating, and he is always fun to be around. When he enters a room, his playful energy fills up the space with such lightheartedness that it's contagious. He's also an excellent storyteller and very animated. If he laughs, you laugh; if he dances, you want to dance. My second brother is very different. An old soul, quiet, and introspective by nature, he often keeps to himself. He is a grounded individual who makes an effort to be aware of the needs of others and gives selflessly of himself without being asked.

From a very young age, my second brother took on the role of caretaker and protector of Mami and me. He was detached from his father and very protective of Mami: the polar opposite of our oldest brother. It was as if each brother had picked a favorite parent and then defended their chosen parent at all costs. There was a lot of tension, hostility, and competition between my two oldest brothers growing up. Their interactions were always subtly intense and could instantly go from sibling camaraderie to rivalry. Their battles often quickly escalated from simple sparks to full-blown fireworks. My fear was always that they would harm one another physically; that's how venomous their exchanges could be.

Their volcanic eruptions mainly happened because my oldest brother was insecure and self-centered. Like his father, he had a grandiose sense of entitlement and poor impulse control. When he didn't get his way, he became explosive and created conflicts that unglued the family. Their battles were mainly over petty things. For example, they once argued because my oldest brother wanted my second brother's share of bacon, though he had already had his share. Another time, they argued because my oldest brother wanted to take my second brother's bike. When he couldn't take it, he tried to destroy the bike with a hammer.

Then there were scarier moments. When my oldest brother got involved in gangs, Mami had to send him out of the country for his protection. Leaving my second brother, at a very young age, alone to fend for himself and to protect us as well. Given his caretaking nature, my second brother stepped up to be the man of the family even though he was just a little boy. In his childhood experience, not only did his father disappoint him, but his older brother failed him as well.

Our home often felt like a minefield, as if one wrong step could result in an explosion. We all walked on eggshells, and poor Mami was often caught in the middle of their war, forever defending my second brother because she knew that my oldest brother was usually in the wrong. He often displaced his internalized anger and frustration onto his younger brother. It often seemed like my mother favored her second-born son. Perhaps she did, but who could blame her? Even in his youth, he always made it a point to take care of her. It makes sense that she would take special care of him too.

My third brother is the product of both fallacy and fear. His father was also no angel, also an addict, and abusive towards my brothers. Mami says he was ignorant and jealous of my older brothers' father and displaced his negative feelings onto his sons. His relationship with Mami did not last long.

He was a dick! However, my youngest brother had the only father in our family who was somewhat present physically, and his father always provided financially for his child. My brother naively thought that this somehow made him better than the rest of us. Unfortunately, my mother contributed to this mindset by showing him special treatment, such as sometimes feeding him better food than the rest of us (this inevitably contributed to his life-long struggle with obesity and his sense of entitlement). My youngest brother was arrogant and ignorant, treating us all like second-class citizens simply because he had a physically present father. His disdain towards us was blatant. He was often disrespectful and dismissive. However, he could only treat my older brothers like this up to a certain point and then he backed off because they would either threaten or outright beat him up. I suffered more because I was a girl and the youngest sibling, and his hostility towards me was worse. My brother had a profoundly ingrained resentment towards me because I displaced him as the baby of the family. Sadly, this dynamic and his general hate and distrust towards women, in general, seem to continue to impede our ability to be genuinely close.

Though he won't admit it, my youngest brother has lived life from a space of fear. By mid-adolescence, he was severely overweight. His doctors told him he would probably die within a few short years. I'm not sure if this was a scare tactic by the doctors or not, but the result was that my brother believed he was going to die, and so he lived in fear for years. However, when the doctor's prediction didn't pan out, my brother declared himself "The Golden Child" (his words, not mine). His sense of entitlement and mistaken false belief that he was better than everyone else increased exponentially. Though, as an adult, I understand his way of being in a psychologically defensive position against the realities of his life, it was nevertheless challenging to live with someone that was often hostile and angry.

The relationship I had with my father was relatively non-existent. I was just two years old when my parents separated. My dad was an overly sensitive and emotionally unstable individual. He was also immature, impulsive, and often exhibited horrendous judgment. While he could be playful, kind, loving, and compassionate, he was also reckless and an addict across many spheres (drugs, gambling, sex), your garden-variety deadbeat dad. He would disappear for long periods, but he would act like nothing was wrong when he showed up again. I remember he came by our house once when my mom was at work, and without her permission, he got into her bed and took a nap as if he was in his own home! As an eight-year-old child, I was just happy that he was home. When Mami got home from work, she unleashed a barrage of insults on him and threw him out of the house. I remember being so hurt and sad over her reaction. I was so confused. I was afraid he would never return and was so angry at mom for chasing him away. I wondered how she could throw him out? As an adult, I can see now that she was calling him out on his audacious behavior and setting a clear boundary (he had no boundaries).

After this incident, I only saw my dad a handful of times. At some point later, he disappeared and was missing for a long time. He became sick and struggled with neurological problems of unknown etiology. My paternal uncle eventually found him in a homeless shelter and cared for him until his death. Ultimately, my dad succumbed to heavy drug use. I was 15 years old when he died. At the time of his death, I was not overwhelmed by grief. I was mentally prepared for his death because he was sick for so long. In retrospect, I realize that his death didn't impact me significantly at the time because he was never the father figure in my internal world; that role belongs solely to my second oldest brother.

Our Sibling Dynamics

By the time I came along, my brothers were nine, seven, and five years old. By then, they were like the "Three Musketeers," a little boy gang that girls were not allowed in! Try as I might, they would not let me join their boys' club. While they would let me play with them sometimes, it was always clear that I was not one of them, which made me mad! This treatment had a lot of meaning at many different levels. First, I was too young to be "one of them." They had developed a special bond between them long before I was born. So even though I was family, I was like an outsider. Second, they were all boys, and I was a girl. In our family and community, boys had more intrinsic value than girls because, as in many cultures in the world, traditional Puerto Rican culture values males much more than females.

To make things worse, Mami gave my brothers special treatment. They didn't have to do chores; I did. They could go outside and play with their friends; I couldn't. She put them in extracurricular activities, not me. My brothers had "Boy Privilege," and I was jealous. I envied them and hated the special treatment they got. Yet, I also adored them and admired them. I wanted to be with them and be like them. Try as I may, I could never quite fit in. Looking back now, I can see and appreciate how the confusing and complicated nature of my relationships with my brothers contributed to the development of who I am today.

There were even more specific conflicts and dynamics at play between each brother and me. My oldest brother, with his chauvinistic mentality, often treated me like I was his slave. While Mami did not intercede to help me, my second-born brother did, which created even more hostility between my oldest two brothers. My second brother took it upon himself to be my caretaker from a very early age. He played with me, took me to school, did homework with me. He was the only father figure I knew, always protecting me, making me feel safe. He took on the role of parenting me when Mami was too exhausted to do it.

While his heart and his intentions were good and honorable, he was still a child playing an adult role and thus made some critical mistakes with me. For example, his expectations of me were often too high, and he made his disappointment quite clear when I did not meet them. These moments were devastating for me and probably contributed to some of my perfectionistic tendencies. Aside from Mami, he was the only other person I never wanted to disappoint. I only remember truly disappointing him one time, but his reaction was so strong that, unbeknownst to him, it reinforced the message that I (my decisions, my actions, my way of being) was not good enough.

My youngest brother was very different. He made sure that I always felt his disdain for me, and he bullied me constantly throughout my childhood. He broke my dolls, mocked and teased me, and sometimes even hit me. Our mutual hostility was palpable. We became each other's figurative and literal punching bags. The sibling dynamics at play in my nuclear family were as powerful.

Our Nuclear Family and Home Life

Living with my brothers and Mami was often difficult. First, I didn't fit in with my mom's concept of Latina. Then, I didn't fit in with the boys. My experiences within my nuclear family were hard to understand, navigate and manage. My family was like a giant jigsaw puzzle, with many pieces and hard to put together. I often did not know or understand what was happening, but I could feel the turmoil and tension in the air. I experienced so much confusion and many mixed emotions throughout my childhood. My young, impressionable mind was constantly absorbing chaos, toxicity, and rejection. A lot of the distress I experienced as a child was the direct result of the madness that at times took place within my nuclear family, as described above. There was individual suffering, like my oldest brother getting involved in gangs, and my mother reengaging in abusive relationships with one addict after another. Collectively, all of us were living in a poor, hostile, drug-infested community, alienated from and rejected by our extended family. My sense of belonging, self-worth, and understanding of my core self was compromised by my childhood experiences.

For a long time, I felt lost and confused in my nuclear family. However, as I got older, I eventually figured out what to do to "survive" (I don't use this word lightly). I understood that the ties that bound us together were stronger than the dynamics and conflicts that made us act crazy towards one another. Despite our differences, my brothers and I understood that it was us, our nuclear family, against the world. We knew that Mami was the black sheep of her family of origin because she was a single mom who had a voice and was not afraid to use it and that we, by default, were considered less important than the other children in our extended family. Our relatives made it clear to us that we were not good enough in their eyes.

Their hostility towards us was sometimes subtle and, at other times, overt. Because of their animosity towards us, we became very protective of one another. It became us against the world. We became like a gang that very few people could infiltrate; this holds true to this day. So, while my nuclear family drove me crazy, they were also all I had, and they meant everything to me.

My experiences with my family were complex and confusing. But this was the environment in which I was reared and socialized, and the context within which I learned to engage with the world. The dynamics that ruled my early life negatively impacted how I interacted with others and caused me to misperceive things. I experienced everything through a filter of hostility and rejection.

I naturally became combative, defiant, and demanding as I learned to navigate through my hostile environment. Challenging the status quo became second nature to me. I couldn't accept the "You ain't nothing but a girl. Stay in your lane" world. I had to act up and speak my truth.

Part II – Me, My Way

My Community

My Puerto Rican home and neighborhood were both intense and flavorful. My brothers and I were all born and raised in the Bronx. There is no other place like it, in both good and bad ways. On a positive note, the culture of the Boogie Down Bronx has a flavor like no other. If you're from the BX, there's an edge and a spiciness to you that everyone recognizes. This sprinkle of allure and spiciness in everyone's personality there is a good thing. However, the overall culture of the Bronx is riddled with anger, frustration, and hostility for a variety of reasons, among them: overcrowding, poverty, racism, sexism, sub-hazard living conditions, crime, drugs, gang violence, etc. Like our home life, the community we were raised in was harsh and severe.

The community I grew up in was predominantly Puerto Rican, Dominican, and Black, and there was clear antagonism between the cultures. I wasn't liked by many of my peers simply because I was Puerto Rican. I also was unpopular because I was never allowed outside to hang out on the block with them. While most of the neighborhood kids hung out in front of the building, Mami would not allow me to because she felt it was inappropriate for a girl to be outside like one of the boys. My neighborhood peers interpreted this as "She thinks she's better than us," and were therefore hostile towards me. The truth was that I wanted to hang out with them. I tried to connect to outsiders in a way I could not connect to my family at home. Unfortunately, I was on lockdown because I was a girl, and I could not hang out with them. They didn't know this, so they resented and ostracized me. Consequently, I didn't have any friends in my neighborhood. Once again, I received the message loud and clear that I did not belong and was not accepted as I was.

It feels overwhelmingly sad and frustrating for a young, developing girl to receive the message that she's not good enough, that she doesn't belong, and that whatever she's doing is wrong. I had no choice but to develop a thick skin and adapt to my environment. I had to learn not to succumb to the overwhelming sadness, frustration, and anger I felt more often than not. I also had to develop coping strategies to help me navigate through the quagmire called my life. Figuring this process out ultimately led me to the strategies I will share with you later.

Adolescence: The Emergence of Me, My Way

Because of everything going on in the outside world around me, my inner world was also in acute upheaval. I entered adolescence with a lot of drama, both externally and internally. I was insecure and struggled with anxiety and depression, experiencing all of the angst of a typical adolescent. I felt like the world didn't understand me and like I didn't fit in. I was also struggling to manage many personal conflicts:

- The domestic violence in my home
- The substance abuse in my family, extended and immediate
- The abandonment and abuse by my sometimes-in, sometimes-out, deadbeat dad
- Dysfunctional interpersonal relationships
- Poverty

By early adolescence, I had decided that everyone was crazy: my family, my peers, my community, me. Nothing made sense to me. The only thing I knew with certainty was that we were all crazy. Living with my nuclear family and observing our madness was intense. We were all struggling with some form of anxiety, depression, and addictions either to food (Mami, my youngest brother, me) or drugs (my two oldest brothers). Everything could be calm one minute, and the next minute, if someone got angry, the rage, violence, and chaos would consume us. My home life was riddled with domestic violence. My brothers were constantly arguing and threatening to beat each other up, quite often brawling like they were strangers fighting in the street. Mami was often trying to separate people. I was constantly being told what to do by everyone and threatened with possible bodily harm if I talked back. There were many times when Mami even played us one against the other. She would instigate the conflict, especially when she was frustrated and overwhelmed and wanted one of us to defend her position. My home life was like a minefield, and you had to tiptoe around and try to be safe. To live safely at our home, you had to learn to avoid the landmines. Survival was the name of the game, not just for Mami, but for the entire family.

We all learned our ways to cope and survive. Because I was a thinker and observer by nature, I constantly tried to make sense of everything. I tried to figure things out in my family, in my community, and ultimately find my place in the world. Looking back, I now know that I was figuring out what I had to do to be safe and escape unscathed, no matter the situation. I am pragmatic by nature, and this seemed like a logical way to navigate through the confusion and messiness in my life. Eventually, I unconsciously decided that life is like a game, and I had to figure out the rules and learn how to play the game. My thinking was not very sophisticated given my age, but this was my new life strategy: the only way to survive (and hopefully not get hurt) was to figure out what was going on and then strategically plan my moves. Maybe because I was a child, I perceived things as a game, even the chaos in my life. Like every child, I always wanted to win the game. Being the youngest child and the only female among my siblings, I learned to be competitive early on, and the value of winning whatever game I was playing.

The Game, The Rules, The Strategies

Figuring out the rules (spoken and not) and the strategies to win the game became the frame I operated from in all areas of my life. No matter what situation presented itself, first, I would observe. Then, I would process what I was taking in and decide how to move forward. Even though every scenario was a new game, my approach was always the same: understand the game, decipher the rules, strategize, then play to win.

Before moving on, I need to explain how I see rules so you can better understand why I appreciate them and how I use them to navigate through all areas of my life. There are fundamental guides and structure-rules, laws, boundaries, and understandings in society that everyone needs to respect and abide by. Many people have a natural aversion to rules. No one likes to be told what to do or how to do things, not even children. But the reality is that we need rules. They provide structure and a general framework that informs us what is acceptable and what is not. For the most part, rules keep people safe. Rules safeguard us against chaos and hedonism. They prevent confusion and provide a common ground and framework, so we can all be on the same page. In life, many people waste valuable time trying to break the rules or challenge them, which can be a waste of one's time, energy, and resources.

I like rules. They help me make sense of things and navigate through life. By adolescence, I had figured out the general rules in my family, community, and school. More importantly, I had started to develop my own general set of rules that I would use to live life my way. I now know that my current concept of the strategies I live by (and teach anyone who will listen!) were formulated in my early youth.

First Spoken Truth

For most of my early life, I remained on the sidelines. To be safe, I stayed to myself and was generally quiet; this wasn't my natural disposition, but I was quickly shut down and put in my place the few times I spoke up about things. I was told to be quiet, that I was a child, and that I didn't know anything. To survive, I learned to keep my thoughts and observations to myself. Although I had learned to keep quiet, in my head, I was often thinking, "I have something to offer!" Adults sometimes make things too complicated. Adults often don't see the obvious, or they don't want to accept the truth. Children are not as guarded, defended, or complicated as adults. They are often brilliant, open, and candid. Children speak their truths and don't see anything wrong; they don't know about being socially appropriate. I was no different. Like most people, I tried to speak my truth since early childhood, but I was stifled and repeatedly wronged for doing so.

I can recall the first time I challenged this silencing and defended myself and my truth. I was about 15, and although I don't remember the details, I remember the experience. Mami and I were arguing about me doing or wearing something outside. Mami worried, "What are the neighbors gonna say?" I vividly remember feeling frustrated and confused. I knew our family hated the neighbors and that they hated us in return. It didn't make sense to me that their opinion would in any way matter in anything pertaining to us. Mami, like most people, was often preoccupied with appearances. Not me. At that point in my life, I was tired of "faking the funk" and acquiescing. In my full adolescent bravado, I challenged Mami, saying, "To hell with the neighbors! They don't like us, and we don't like them, so who cares what they think?" It was the first time I was truly defiant towards Mami. It was the first time I openly voiced what I was thinking and feeling without regard for consequences. It was the first time I spoke my truth, challenging the status quo. It was scary, but also empowering and liberating, and it was a pivotal moment for me. I believe this was the moment when I made the internal decision to be Me: to live my truth and to do things my way. It felt like I was released from some metaphoric prison where I had been bound by people-pleasing, as if a huge weight had been lifted off me, and I could now freely be myself. It was the first time in my life that I truly stood up for what I believed. It was the first time I openly demonstrated that I believed in Me and my right and determination to live life my way.

Flair and Flamboyance (Oh Boy, Was I Loud)

This new ability to express my individuality openly and freely resulted in the evolution of an interesting adolescent and young adult who was flavorful. Two major things were occurring concurrently. First, I was becoming more confident and defining myself as I saw fit. I was done with being stifled. By late adolescence, I had developed my style. I dressed however I wanted. One day, I would look like all the other people in my neighborhood with the baggy jeans and construction boots, the next day I would be in full 80s Madonna mode. The day after that, I would be in full cowgirl regalia with the fringes and cowboy hat in the middle of the ghetto. For sure, I had swag, a flavor, and spice that was specific to me. I was free and expressing "ME," and I didn't care what anyone thought about how I dressed or who I was. I had learned to live with rejection, so I did things and wore things, and acted in ways that fit my evolving personality. I was not a total rebel. Rather, instead of focusing on fitting in or going against the mainstream, I focused on expressing my individuality. Some people said that I was "EXTRA," that I was too much or flamboyant, but I didn't care. When you choose to live in your truth and essence instead of acquiescing to the norm, some people will inevitably perceive you negatively and judge you for being different. When I think of how I carried myself then, I can see that I was extra loud, extra gregarious, extra flamboyant, extra obnoxious at times, extra competitive, etc. I know my "extraness" was my way of declaring my individuality and voice to the world. After years of feeling suppressed, I was determined to be seen and heard!

Figuring Out My Game

The second major thing that was occurring is that I was figuring out "the game" I wanted to play in my life. I was developing my brand of the game. For Mami, survival was the name of the game; she taught me that I had to play the game better than she did. She told me not to repeat her mistakes and make sure that I always aimed to do better than she did and be a better woman. Mami often said, "I work hard in a factory, so that you don't have to. Go to school. Don't be like me." Or she would say, "Only have kids with one man; look at all the problems we have because of all the mixed blood in our family" (Mami thought the reason we fought so much was that we had different fathers, bloodlines, and genetics in one nuclear family). Mami was always teaching me her strategies on how to live. She talked to me about how to save money, how to manage a home, how to be a wife, etc. (the "classic Latina" stuff), so that I would have the tools to make it in this cold, cruel world. In retrospect, I can see that Mami provided me with the rules for her survival game. She was giving me the strategies that she had figured out. She often told me of her pitfalls, so I could avoid them. Mami was helping me figure out my own game, and she was doing her best to make sure that I played a better game than she did and did all I could to be the best at my game. She has no idea of the ultimate impact she had in helping me become who I am, or how grateful I will always be to her.

Taking in everything Mami taught me, I then figured out the basic rules of My game. Whereas Mami's game was to survive, my game became to thrive; surviving was not enough. I needed to do better than Mami; she demanded it, and I wanted it. Ultimately, I had three simple rules: speak your truth, be yourself, and trust your instincts. These were the unwritten guidelines that I set up for myself to live life my way.

The World of Academia

By 16, I had figured out I was really good at school, and this wasn't always the case. When I first entered grade school, I was put in the lowest level class because I did not speak English. The teachers mistakenly thought I was dumb just because of the language barrier, but I proved them wrong by fifth grade. By then, I was in the top class. By the age of 10, I had figured out the rules to this school thing! I was smart. I liked the mental challenge that school provided me. More importantly, school was the first place where I experienced a sense of competence, where I was really good at something, and where someone (a teacher) truly saw me for who I was and made me feel good about myself. The sense of accomplishment I felt due to my academic achievements was exhilarating, as was the much-needed understanding, approval, and acceptance I felt for who I was becoming at my core. School provided me with the stomping grounds where I could truly and creatively express myself. School became my favorite game, and I was winning.

High School: Ms. R and Psychology

I went to one of the worst high schools in the Bronx, William H. Taft High School (it's not even a regular high school anymore)! It was a rough environment, but I am grateful for the two main things I got out of that school: my first true mentor, my English teacher, Ms. Denise Rodriguez, and my career path.

Ms. R

Ms. Rodriguez, or Ms. R as I called her, was a tough and spicy Puerto Rican woman that had bravado and lived in her essence. When I once said to her, "Ms. R, you have to…," she stopped me dead in my tracks and replied, "I don't have to do anything except be Puerto Rican and die." [Drop the mic]. She was feisty, and I loved and respected her. She stood her ground no matter what. I first met her when she taught my tenth-grade honors English class. By the end of the first marking period, Ms. R made a list of the students who would fail because they were not working at a level that merited being in the honors program. She presented this list to the department chairman and informed him of her intention to fail these students if they did not improve their work. She got a lot of pushback from her department. They told Ms. R that she could not fail that many students because that would considerably shrink the honors program. Her answer was, "They're failing themselves. I'm not going to pass them if they have not earned it." She was passionate about her work and had a degree of integrity that I try to model to this day. Those students on her list did indeed fail her class and were dropped from the honors program. Ms. R weeded out the dead weight and reestablished the integrity of the honors program. Ms. R was not afraid to stand up for what she believed. She modeled for me that you get what you work for, and that everyone has to put in the effort. Ms. R had a strong work ethic, just like Mami. Although I never thought of this as a child, Ms. R's inner strength and integrity reminded me of Mami.

Ms. R was my first role model outside of my family. Once, after a visit to my home and a long conversation with my mother, Ms. R told me, "Your mother doesn't know you at all." At the time, I didn't know why she said this, and I was confused. But this memory stayed with me because it was the first time someone openly voiced and understood what I was experiencing. Ms. R recognized that Mami did not see or understand who I truly was. That insight was invaluable to me. Ms. R contributed significantly to my overall development across many areas. She showed me how to love myself. She taught me to respect myself. She helped me grow, expand, and stretch beyond the confines of societal and cultural limits and expectations. She helped me learn to be comfortable in my skin simply by being who she was.

Ms. R was a true treasure for me. She came into my life exactly when I needed her to. She opened my eyes to possibilities that I had never conceived. By simply being herself, she helped me tweak and develop some of my rules and strategies, and she helped me play this game called life a little bit better. Had I not gone to this crazy high school, I would have never met her.

Ms. R was more than my teacher; she was like family. We got so close that I even visited her home and spent time with her family. Being part of her family life was priceless for me. I got to experience what a healthy marriage and family life was like by observing her and the relationship she had with her husband, Big Red, as I called him. Her husband was a tall, white man with blazing red hair, not your typical-looking Puerto Rican. He looked enormous next to her small stature. She was petite with caramel-colored skin and dark hair. They could not have been more different in their appearances. Their love, passion, respect, and adoration for one another were beautiful to witness, and there was a deep, spiritual connection to their union. Theirs seemed a match made in heaven. Their bond and union set the standard for me of how a healthy and divinely ordained relationship should look.

Their relationship also set the standard for what I wanted. So much so, that when I was ready to get married, a little more than a decade after I graduated high school, I took my husband-to-be to meet Ms. R and Big Red. I did not want to get married without them meeting him first, and although I had not spoken to or seen them since high school, I felt compelled to see them and get their approval. When we visited Ms. R and Big Red, we had a most pleasant time. I did not share with Ms. R or Big Red that I came seeking their approval and blessing to get married. We enjoyed a beautiful afternoon and laughed and bonded. When the time came for us to say our goodbyes, Ms. R came up to my side of the car as Big Red gave my then-fiancé directions. She stared into my eyes, smiled broadly, nodded her head, and amazingly said, "Yes." Without me asking for it overtly, she gave me the approval I had needed. Ms. R knew I had come seeking her blessing to get married. I will forever remember Ms. R as one of the true blessings I received at Taft High School.

Psychology

The second blessing that my high school provided me with was my career choice. In 11th grade, our school offered a special elective, a class in psychology, to our honors class. I had never heard of psychology or therapy. As I sat in class and listened, I absorbed everything the teacher said, and I was in awe, as it was all new to me. This foreign material was fascinating, and I was beyond intrigued. This psychology class opened up a whole new world for me: an entirely new perspective through which I could comprehend my experiences. I began to understand some of the dynamics at play in my family and my life. The information validated my internal belief that I wasn't the problem. It also opened my eyes to the reality that we ALL were suffering.

In this class, I learned that we humans make ourselves nuts trying to fit in and be "normal." This insight was the first time I realized that people make themselves feel crazy by trying to be like everyone else instead of being who they genuinely are. I realized that there wasn't necessarily anything wrong with anyone per se, but that there was definitely something wrong with the families, cultures, and communities that push us to behave in rigid, specific, acceptable ways, even if those ways don't resonate with who we intrinsically are. I finally understood that we all experience some form of disconnect from ourselves, our families, and society, and that we are all searching for a sense of belonging and for meaning and purpose.

This revelation lifted a huge weight off my shoulders. For the first time, I didn't feel alone. I realized everyone struggles with feeling different or not fitting in with their family or community. I finally understood some of the chaos at play in my life. I never spoke to the teacher about my personal experiences. Still, that one high school psychology class provided me with a new lens through which I could process and better understand my family, my experiences, and people in general. It opened my eyes to the complexities of the human psyche and how thoughts and beliefs impact how we behave, engage with the world, and live our lives. I was hooked! I was excited and eager to learn more, thrilled with the possibility of this being my profession. I could breathe a sigh of relief because I now had a direction, a foundation on which I could build my life.

As I neared the end of high school and my adolescence, I was in a good place. I had become a more confident individual. I was making efforts to live my truth. I was successful academically. I was a good person. I was figuring out this game called life, and I was doing it well. For the most part, life was good, and I was riding a wave of excitement and a sense of invincibility that is common to youth. In school, I worked at being the best. I was dedicated and determined to succeed. Going to college and graduate school became the natural course of action for me.

Adulthood: Riding the Wave

My 20s were all about solidifying this persona that surfaced in late adolescence. I did my best to live true to who I was at the time. I was bold, loud, flamboyant, and confident. I pursued what was important to me and what interested me, and I worked hard to achieve what I wanted. I became a vibrant adult who was excited about life and all the possibilities it offered. I went to college and then graduate school, worked, partied, and came into my own. I was self-assured. I did well professionally and began to develop a career in a field I loved that fascinated me. I was at the top of my game. I had figured out the rules of this game called life, and I was doing well. I was honoring my true essence as best as I could, and my overall growth was a testament to this.

The Relationship

I worked hard during this period of my life. I went to school full-time, worked full-time, and I partied hard. My favorite pastime then was going clubbing with friends, and the hotspot was Webster Hall in Manhattan. I went every weekend and let loose. Given everything on my plate, I had little time to relax. So, the nights I went to Webster Hall were rare moments I could be entirely free, even if only for a few hours, and forget about all the responsibilities I had.

It was at this club that I met and eventually fell in love with my future husband. He was unlike any other man I had ever met, a man who seemed to have a spirit and a spunk quite similar to mine. I loved how he honored his truth and how different he was from everyone I knew. He was like a breath of fresh air. He seemed to be free, and he lived life his way. There were not a lot of pretenses, he was who he was. Take it or leave it! We had a whirlwind romance. It felt like being in his presence somehow validated my right to be me.

Unfortunately, I did not see back then that a part of me still sought external approval. I wanted to be accepted as I was, and seeing this reflection of me, in male form, somehow supported or endorsed me. In my early adulthood, I was blind to the underlying dynamic at play in my psyche (given my upbringing) that perhaps a male version of me was *better or more acceptable* than the female version of me. My unconscious need for approval undermined my true power. I would come to learn in time that only I can validate my right to be.

Our relationship evolved quickly, and there was a true connection between us. We were kindred spirits and felt right together. However, even early on, something seemed off. I saw it, but I ignored it. Perhaps we were too much alike and didn't balance each other out. Maybe we were both too emotionally and psychologically immature or injured to be in a healthy relationship. I can now see that his overall dysfunction was familiar territory, so similar to my family of origin, it felt like a comfortable old blanket. I knew how to navigate through chaos and conflict quite well. Our psychological narratives were too similar. It was a recipe for disaster, but I wanted this relationship to work. I was committed to it even though my inner knowing was screaming for me to bail. In this

26

relationship, I did not play by the rules of my own game for the first time in a long time. I did not follow my intuition, I did not always speak my truth, and I was not true to myself. I neglected to follow the rules of my game consistently. I certainly should have known that there was no way I could triumph if I wasn't being my genuine self. Apparently, I had to learn this lesson the hard way.

The Power Struggle, The Chaos

Like all dysfunctional relationships, ours was messy. I don't need to discuss everything that went wrong between us because there is no power or integrity in blaming, finger-pointing, or victimizing. However, I want to point out that there were real power struggles both between us and within each of us. Our external struggles as a couple were derivative of our individual struggles. Looking back, I can see that deep down, neither of us knew who we were or what we wanted. We were young and naive, and we didn't notice we were mirroring each other's turmoil. Each of us was still speaking our truth, but how we expressed it changed. We went from a space of love, support, and understanding to one of anger, venom, and hurt. At some point, it seemed like we were shoving our truths down each other's throats. Therein was the power struggle between us. You might think that this would have been enough for us to throw in the towel and walk away, but it wasn't. Something kept us together. I believe that our Soul love for one another was genuine. It was the glue that kept us holding on to a relationship that no longer worked or served us.

Despite the apparent chaos that defined our relationship, we trudged on. We did it all. We got married, got the dog, had the kids, bought the house. It wasn't all bad. There were good moments, but they became fewer and fewer and farther apart. As things deteriorated between us, instead of following my gut instinct (and my rules in my game of life), I tried to follow Mami's advice to fight for my marriage and family. I tried not to repeat the cycle of broken relationships and single parenting. Throughout the years, like Mami, I used my faith to keep me above water: my faith in God and the goodness of all people. My hope was that my partner would meet me in the middle, and we would figure things out together. Sadly, as my daughter later told me, when things finally fell apart, I let my faith blind me to the reality of what was happening in our home and family. She could see I was holding on to a relationship that no longer worked. The man I had fallen in love with was long gone. I was letting my blind faith in her father and hope for our relationship keep me hostage in a chaotic, disorganized, and dysfunctional relationship. My daughter was young, but oh so perceptive and accurate.

The Lesson

I realized something monumentally important in the demise of this relationship. Once it came to a crashing halt and I had the opportunity to reflect on all that had transpired, I had to face the overwhelming reality that I had long ago lost the connection to my true self in my efforts to save our marriage. Though losing a long-term relationship and my family as I knew it were painful experiences, nothing was sadder to me than the reality that I had lost touch with the confident, self-assured, and rich individual I once was. In trying to save my relationship and my family, I had lost myself!

There is nothing worse than being disconnected from oneself, and nothing is more spiritually painful than no longer honoring your truth and inner knowing. Over the years, I had slowly acquiesced to things in my marriage that did not speak to my truth, trying to appease my former spouse. Even sadder, every time I did it, I knew I was doing it and felt the inner turmoil that takes place when you're being ingenuine to yourself. Whenever I gave in to something I did not genuinely agree with, I rationalized my actions and quieted the internal dialogue that screamed out, "You're a fraud!" Mami watched me struggle, but she could not help. She did not understand my process. She would have walked away long before I did. I felt so alone.

For a long time, I was not being true to my core beliefs and principles. I know why I did it. I was trying to keep my marriage intact. I was trying to do better than Mami had. But inevitably, I failed. The end did not justify the means. I worked hard to salvage my marriage at the expense of my well-being. There's no way this could have ever worked out in the long run. It is unfortunate that in trying to hold on to something that I truly valued, my marriage and family, I lost something I valued more: myself. In retrospect, I guess I had to learn firsthand that there is nothing more important or valuable than having a genuine connection to yourself and honoring it. The words "To thine own self be true" should be everyone's mantra.

The realization that I had compromised my integrity to myself was not only sad, but also embarrassing and humiliating. My life's work was about helping people be honest with themselves and move in the direction of living in their truths. How could I have allowed myself to get so far removed from my own truth? What happened to me? I lost my focus until what mattered was a blur. Being genuine to myself and living my truth had fallen by the wayside. Somewhere in the process, I stopped playing my game, my way. I stopped fighting for what I wanted. I stopped fighting to be seen and heard. I gave up and gave in. I got caught up in the pretense, in the "fake it to you make it" mentality. Nothing good can ever come from being fraudulent in any way. Many painful experiences, not just for me, but also for my children and entire family, were the price I had to pay for not honoring my truth.

I learned the hard way the importance and the necessity of speaking and living my truth. But I still believe that everything happens for a reason. I believe that my life, my marriage, my family, all of it, had to implode so that I could wake up and once again start honoring my truth. For a very long time, I was not living in my truth or my purpose. The end of my marriage and my family as I knew it felt like a crashing wave that wiped me out. It turned my life upside down. Fortunately, it also reminded me of God's plan for me. My life's work has always been about service to others, and though I was serving others through my clinical work, I realized that I was playing this particular game on way too small of a scale, and way too safely. The crashing wave that rocked my life to its core helped me face the reality that it was time for me to play a bigger game. I now know that I have to share my knowledge and experiences on a larger scale to make a real difference in my life and the lives of others. The time has come for me to step out of my comfort zone, play bigger, and speak and live my truth.

Part III – Guidelines to Keep in Mind

What I Learned

I stated at the very beginning that I felt compelled to share my story. I felt an internal pressure to give a voice to what I had experienced and learned. Initially, my desire to put pen to paper was primarily fueled by my need to write and talk about what I had gone through. I needed to tell my story, to write my truth. As I wrote, though, I became acutely aware that I also needed to tell my story so that anyone going through something similar does not feel alone or ashamed of their process. I hoped that by sharing my vulnerability, I could make it easier for others to share theirs. The deeper I got into my story, the more hopeful I became that sharing my experiences and what I learned from them could help others avoid making mistakes similar to those I made. In the end, the desire to tell my story became more about sharing what I have learned from it and the tools and techniques I use to help others live in their authenticity. These are the same strategies I used in my personal life initially to survive and now to thrive.

I've shared that I experienced extensive chaos and suffering in my youth. Like everyone else who experiences abuse, is neglected or traumatized, I learned to cope in my way. My early life was overwhelmingly challenging for me, and I had to develop strategies to manage all the challenges and conflicts I was exposed to and subjected to. I learned how to adapt quickly and survive among all the dysfunction in my home and community. Without realizing it then, probably because I was so young, I developed an internal working model that viewed life as a game. This model simplified things for me as a child and probably brought some levity to my life. As a kid, I turned every situation I found myself in into figuring out what game I was playing, what the rules of this particular game were, and then developing strategies that would help me win the game. Maybe because I was a child, I perceived things as a game, even the chaos in my life. Like every child, my desire and intention were always to win the game. Being the youngest child and the only female among my siblings, I learned to be competitive and value winning whatever game I was playing.

Though I viewed my experiences in this game-like manner, there is no doubt that in reality, I was trying to manage all the chaos and dysfunction in my life. I was trying to survive. As a child, I often felt threatened and in danger. My strategies for survival and for winning the game were organized and structured responses to trauma. This sounds sad and scary, and it was. However, from these unfortunate circumstances evolved my perspective that life is a game, and also evolved the strategies I teach others and try to live by consistently.

This perspective remains my frame for life. I operate as if everything is a game: work, parenting, relationships, etc. Over time, I've learned to refine and redefine my game, and the strategies I'm about to share continue to serve me well. I hope that the guidelines I follow in my day-to-day life and use with my clients will also help you become more empowered and better at playing your own game, that is, at speaking and living your truth. Before we begin to look at the strategies I'm about to outline, you need some background information to guide you in appreciating and optimizing the value of these techniques fully.

My Perception Is My Reality

First, let's talk about our understanding of "our truth." "Our truth" is a concept. It is relative. While the absolute truth is what happened, the concrete/factual experience, "our truth," is our version, our story, of what happened. What we perceive as "our truth" is a compromise between reality and the filter through which we take in what happened. "Our filter" is our particular way of taking things in based on our experiences and our belief systems. Our filter colors our perception.

I have a friend that always says, "My perception. My Reality." Truer words were never spoken; we all engage with the world based upon our perceptions of the world. The challenge for us all is in accepting that perception is individualistic. We all have our own way of perceiving things based on our past experiences, and we often forget that others see things differently. Therein is the foundation for misperception and miscommunication. We all tend to hold on to our perceptions and believe that Our Truth is "The Truth." We all need to understand that what is true for us may not be true for others.

The other hurdle that we all face is accepting that our perception and our truth are fluid and can change based on new experiences and understandings, which then creates a new filter through which we take in experiences. Put simply, our truth is relative to where we're at dynamically in any given moment and to what our particular filter is at that point in time. This means that what's true for us now may not necessarily be true for us later. It also means that what is true for us may not be true for others.

Let me give you a simple example. When I was about four years old, my second eldest brother, father figure, protector, and hero did something I will never forget. At that time, we lived in a mouse-infested apartment, so we had a cat that chased mice all the time. I was terrified of mice, and my brother knew this. We were walking into the living room one day, and the cat was running around like a maniac. I remember the room was dark and seemed scary to me. As we quietly approached the entrance to the living room, I could hear the frenzy of the cat in pursuit. My brother protectively placed me behind him as we slowly entered the living room. Suddenly I heard a loud BOOM! and then silence. My brother had stomped on the floor, and then all activity immediately ceased. He had killed the mouse. His stomp jarred me. Yes, because it was unexpected, but more importantly, because it was the first time I experienced my brother, my protector, act aggressively and violently. It was the first time I was ever afraid of him. My perception of him as my safe protector was suddenly overshadowed by the reality that he could be hostile and scary. My perception of him, my truth, shifted in one moment from "he's safe" to "he's dangerous." This was hard for me to take in as it was not how I had experienced him up to that moment.

Years later, as I recounted this story to my therapist, she insisted that I tell her his age at the time of this incident. I did not see the relevance in this, but she was relentless. As we talked, I eventually realized that every time I told this story, I said my "big" brother as if he was all grown up at the time. The reality is that if I was 4, he was only 11, a mere child himself. For years, the story in my head was that he was "big," that a grown-up person had done this scary thing. Yet, the reality was that my brother was a little boy when this happened. I'm focusing on his age because my perception, my truth, of my brother changed based on a "new" piece of information at that moment in therapy. His actual age at the time of this incident versus my perception that he was "big" and "grown." I know this detail seems a bit trivial, but this moment in therapy was the first time in my life that I saw that my truth, my perception, was not always an accurate representation of what happened. "My truth" was nothing more than a narrative based on my experiences and the filter through which I perceived things at that time. I learned in that therapy session that "my truths" are not absolute truths; they're relative truths, not the only truths. This moment in therapy for me was eye-opening. It made me aware that personal truth is relative.

As we begin to speak and live our truth, we have to remain mindful that everyone has their version of personal truth and that their truth is just as important as ours. This realization will perhaps be the most challenging thing for us to keep in mind. We may want to beat others over the head with our truth. We might even want others to accept our truth as "The Truth" to validate our experiences and beliefs. But no one has to validate your truth for it to matter or be real. Always honor your truth and your experiences. But remember that your truth and perceptions can change and evolve as you do. It is an injustice to hold on to old truths and perceptions that no longer serve us. This type of rigidity gets in the way of growth. Be open to new possibilities. You'll be surprised at what becomes available to you when you allow yourself to change the filter through which you perceive the world!

Speaking My Truth vs. Living My Truth

The second guideline I want you to keep in mind is the difference between speaking your truth and living your truth. You might think that speaking your truth and living it are the same, that the two naturally go together. Think about it. If you're brave enough to speak your truth, then living your truth seems to be the logical next step. However, that is not necessarily how things play out. Towards the end of my marriage, I learned firsthand that there are times when we think we're living our truth, but in actuality, we are not. I also learned that there are other times when we even try to convince ourselves that we are living in our truth when we know deep down that we are not, or we come to understand that we're living our truth in some areas of our lives, but not in others.

While I was, for the most part, living my truth at work and with my kids, I was not living it consistently in my marriage or with my larger family. As the demands of daily living increased in my marriage, and as I fought for fairness in the division of labor in our family and home, direct and candid communication and mutual respect became increasingly harder. Old, dysfunctional behavioral patterns consistently resurfaced, which often led to explosive conflicts. Reasserting my boundaries and demanding respect in my marriage and my family was often exhausting. At some points, it was simply easier to give in to the status quo, to "fake the funk," if you will, than it was to keep fighting.

In my life, I have many roles: mother, daughter, sister, aunt, doctor, friend, Latina, woman, athlete, etc. Learning how to manage the many versions of myself cohesively and genuinely has been difficult at times. Sometimes, I dropped the ball and didn't live up to the expectations in each of these roles (for example, when I neglected to support a family member in distress adequately). Then there were times when I intentionally refused to acquiesce to the expectations as a mother, female, or as the youngest child, or as a Latina or whatever! It can be challenging to be genuine to yourself when you feel pressured, internally or externally, to meet or fulfill certain expectations inherent to specific roles. For me, this was complicated. In my family, as a little sister, wife, and mother, I had the unspoken pressure to be a classic Latin female- that is, to marginalize myself and dim my light. The personal challenges I faced were directly related to my not fitting into the preconceived traditional roles (such as Latina women being expected to love all things domestic and defer to male superiority), while also having a feisty spirit and personality that wanted to be seen and heard in its authenticity. Things at times got even more complicated for me because as much as I wanted to be seen for my individuality, in reality, I also wanted to fit in and be a part of the larger group(s).

I worked hard to push through all the spoken and unspoken pressures to be who others expected me to be. I wanted to be me. I wanted to be genuine to my inner self. Sometimes I felt like I had to be over-the-top obnoxious in my personality and behaviors, so that other people would get the point: don't tell me how to be, don't tell me what to do, and don't judge me! At times, it felt like I was beating people over the head with my truth. But this felt necessary because I was often wronged for what I said, how I spoke, or how I acted. I was often ostracized for simply speaking and living my truth.

In reflecting on my overall process and trying to understand my experiences, I can now humbly admit that part of my "in your face, I am who I am" attitude had to do with the reality that as much as I thought I was living and speaking my truth, there were some key areas of my life, like in my marriage, where I was not being genuine to myself. Then there were other areas where I was playing it small and safe, as in my career. Looking back, I believe some of the loudness or obnoxiousness I expressed may have been directly related to trying to convince myself that I was living my truth.

Life has since taught me that it is not necessary to beat others over the head with your truth. It is, however, necessary to live and honor your truth, and you can only do this through your actions. Actions speak louder than words. How you behave speaks louder than anything you say. Your actions will speak your truth, whether you like it or not. It's important to be honest with ourselves and with others about where we stand in the process of living authentically. Quite often, we lie to ourselves regarding how genuine we are being.

This is not helpful. For most of us, figuring out how to live and speak our truth is a lifelong journey. Time and experiences teach us our truth, who we are, and who we are not. As our perceptions of ourselves evolve, so will our truths. Change is inevitable; we need to embrace it. The key to being true to yourself is to remain connected to your inner knowing and to let it guide you towards your greatness. You have to trust that you know yourself better than anyone else does, and that the inner guidance you have is the best instrument to guide you in your journey towards your true self. Trust that Divine part of you. Trust the process.

Speaking and living your truth is an experience that evolves as you continue to grow and change. It is an organic and evolutionary process. The strategies I outline are intended to help you navigate through and facilitate the never-ending self-growth process. They are intended to support your journey as you develop, expand, and step into your unique and Divine Soul purpose.

Part IV – Strategies to Help You Speak and Live Your Truth

Strategy #1: Welcome the Divine

A God of My Understanding

I had an "Ah-ha!" moment many years ago that provided me with the framework for the concept of "A God of My Understanding." Several years ago, I went to my oldest brother's 25th sobriety anniversary. One of the speakers was a woman with over 25 years of sobriety herself. She spoke candidly about her struggles with substance abuse and sobriety. She was engaging and spoke passionately about her experiences and the challenges that continuously tested her sobriety. As I listened to her story, it appeared that despite all of her years of sobriety, she struggled with a lot of unresolved pain and conflict. Intrigued by her story-telling, the psychologist in me focused closely on her words. I soon realized that she kept referring to "a God of my understanding" as she discussed her process and painful experiences. The more she spoke, the clearer it became that she was still grappling with extensive inner turmoil despite her many years of abstaining from drug use. The clinician in me questioned how much of her healing and self-growth work she still had to do.

Absorbed in her story, I listened intently to what she said and what she seemed to be implying. Then it hit me like a lightning bolt. She wasn't just angry about the things that had happened to her. She appeared to be angry at the God of her understanding for letting them happen. The more she spoke, the more I realized that she was still questioning God's process and intent and was mad about how things had or still were transpiring in her life. This woman seemed to be in spiritual turmoil. As she continued to repeat "a God of my understanding," I began to wonder if some of her struggles were related to her still trying to understand the concept of God, Divinity, and a Higher Power, beyond surface levels. I also questioned if part of her distress was about developing further or deepening her relationship with a God of her understanding.

At that moment, I realized that this is probably everyone's experience at some point. Most of us desire a connection to God, the Creator of all things, at some point in our lives. Most of us want a connection to something larger and grander than ourselves. Sadly, many of us don't know how to seek out and develop this relationship. Even more tragic, some of us don't realize that perhaps that is what's missing in our lives. A solid relationship with the Creator can fill that inner void that many of us experience in our lives. When people ask, *"What is the meaning of life?"* for me, the answer is "Connecting to God. Developing a personal relationship with the Creator of all that is, so that we can connect to our true selves and understand our Divine purpose and then do what it is that we were born to do!"

As I listened to this woman repeatedly say, "a God of my understanding," it was clear to me that she seemed to be trying to understand the concept of God in a manner that made sense to her. The passion she spoke with led me to believe that she had faith in the existence of something Divine. She seemed to lack a cohesive understanding of Source Energy and tapping into this Higher Consciousness internally. She had faith in God, but she didn't seem to know how to connect to God. I thought to myself, "This woman's spiritual turmoil could begin to resolve if she had some guidance in exploring her thoughts and beliefs about God." She needed some assistance in expanding and deepening her understanding of the Creator of all that is. As I had this thought, it felt like a veil had lifted. This woman's experience seemed to be living proof of what I knew intuitively. When individuals speak of God, the Creator, Higher Consciousness, Energy, The Universe, Science, etc., they are all talking about the same thing.

At that moment, I understood that our collective ability to discuss, understand, and connect around this Almighty Essence and Presence was being impeded by the reality that we were all speaking a different language of sorts. We did not seem to comprehend that we were discussing the same thing: a God of our understanding. The challenge before us is learning to accept and respect our different perspectives and understandings of The Divine, while embracing our collective belief in this Higher Power.

This moment in a Narcotics Anonymous meeting gave me an epiphany that has transformed how I work, interact with others, and live in my Divinely-Inspired Purpose. Now I understand the essence of my work is to help others connect to and develop a relationship with a God of their understanding, to the Creator of all that is. The work includes embracing and accepting the term "A God of My Understanding," and having dialogues about this amazing Presence and understanding how relating to this Higher Consciousness enriches our lives. For now, our ability to talk about this Source Energy collectively and respectfully is more important than what we call it. The important thing is to acknowledge that something much larger and more powerful than us exists, and accept that if we connect to this Presence, we will never feel alone and will forever be guided in all we do. I believe with my entire being that our overall growth and development is contingent upon us developing a true connection and relationship with a God of our understanding.

Our Journey Towards Believing and Trusting

It is fair to say that we will all struggle with believing in or trusting in God at some point in our lives. I'm no different. I've questioned God many times throughout my life, and I continue to do so when things are unclear. Sometimes things happen that make no sense, unconscionable things that cause immense turmoil and hurt. In these moments, it makes sense that we question why God would allow atrocities to occur, or why we need to experience pain and suffering. These incidents don't make sense to us, but there is a lesson in this for us all. We need to stop viewing God and The Universe through the lens of humanity and expecting things that are Divinely ordered to make sense to us. I believe God has a Divine Plan for us all. I believe there is order in the Universe.

Unfortunately, sometimes our experiences are so negative and overwhelming that we never move past them. We get stuck, doubt God, and we don't understand His/Her plan and intention. We get angry and confused when things don't make sense. Sometimes, we even get lost and feel disconnected from God. When we feel disconnected from God, from our Higher Power, we experience an internal void that nothing but God's essence can again fulfill. Therein begins our true suffering. We all try to fill it with other things. We seek fancy titles, drugs, food, money, sex, material possessions, etc. But nothing can take the place of a Higher Power in our lives. Though it can sometimes be difficult to do so, we have to allow ourselves to trust God and walk by faith, not by sight. If we don't, we will remain stuck in our hurt and suffering and stay derailed in our thoughts and our life journeys.

As we move along this journey called Life, we will encounter hurdles and mountains to climb that seem insurmountable. However horrid, these obstacles and challenges help us understand and prepare us to live in Our Purpose. They prepare us to do the work that God has intended for us to do. Though some of the things that happen make no sense now, we have to trust that everything happens for a reason and there are no coincidences. Everything that happens is Divinely scripted and intentional. We have to trust God always and in all ways!

My Understanding of God

Like most people, my journey towards understanding God and having a relationship to this Higher Power has had vicious pitfalls and dark valleys where I questioned God's reasoning, plan, and intention. I am fortunate. What I have never questioned is God's existence. For this, I humbly thank my mom. She made sure that I understood that God is present in EVERYTHING, especially in moments and events that are hard, dark, or difficult to comprehend or manage. Mami taught me that everything happens for a reason and that although I may not understand what is transpiring at the moment, I have to trust that God knows what S/He is doing. You can only imagine how difficult it was for the rational side of me to accept this thinking. Nonetheless, I trusted Mami, so trust became the core element and foundation for my relationship with God. This lesson is perhaps the most precious gift and the most important thing that Mami taught me. TRUST GOD! No matter what happens. I may not always understand why things happen or agree with how things play out, but I 100% TRUST GOD and His plan for us all.

Please understand that it is okay to struggle with God, question God, and not see the Divinity in all things. We are human beings with minds that want to comprehend and explain things rationally. I believe God wants us to question everything. Why else would God give us the ability to think? However, as humans, we are often limited in our understanding of things that are Divinely orchestrated. In these moments, we have to trust God's process, God's will, and way. I realize that this type of blind faith in God and acceptance of His/Her will is quite difficult, if not impossible, for many people to accept. Many people have lost faith in God or doubt His/Her existence. Yet, most people do believe in something: call it Energy, or Science, or The Universe. I truly believe that at a very basic level, we are all talking about the same thing. We believe that something bigger than us exists and we trust and believe in this larger-than-life Presence, regardless of what we call it. For a while, the warrior, controlling, combative side of me would argue and insist that everyone accept that whatever they called this Presence, we were all indisputably talking about God. Wisely, I have long since stopped trying to push my truth, my perception, onto others. I now understand that we speak different languages, given our diverse backgrounds and experiences. Today, I am more invested in our collective ability to talk about this Almighty Presence, and in helping others develop a true understanding with the God of their understanding. Who or what is your idea of a Higher Power in your life? How does The Divine/God/The Universe manifest itself in your life?

Understanding and Connecting to God, the Creator, and Source Energy

Many of us do not know how to connect to God because the idea of an Almighty Creator was not explained in a meaningful manner. My friend is a pastor, and he says that God and our relationship to God is an Experience, that you feel it, that you have to work at developing a connection and a relationship to God. I cannot tell you how to develop a relationship with a God of your understanding; that's above my paygrade. I am far from an expert in this area. However, I can tell you that it begins simply with being brave enough to start a conversation with a God of YOUR understanding. Try to make it a daily habit to speak openly and directly to your Higher Power. The same way you would speak to your best friend. It's that simple.

People connect to The Creator in their own ways. You must figure out what works best for you. It may be helpful to read and research to expand your knowledge and personal understanding of The Divine. There is an unbelievable amount of information at your fingertips, but you have to actively put in the work to learn about and cultivate a relationship with the Almighty Creator. No one can do this personal work for you, though many can help and guide you. Take the first step; it's usually the hardest. As you put in the effort to develop a personal relationship with a God of your understanding, remember that the beautiful thing about doing your work is that no one can ever take it away from you!

I like to keep things simple. I like to talk a lot, so I speak directly to God; this is how I pray. I have direct conversations with God. Sometimes these dialogues are in my head, and sometimes, they're out loud. Sometimes these conversations take place in the car, the house, or the shower. It doesn't matter where or how they occur; what matters is that they happen all the time. I converse with God every day. I then "listen" to God's response. Listening for a reply is critical. I believe that God communicates with us all, but many don't know how to listen. God always responds to prayers. But some people don't understand that sometimes the answer is "Sorry. No." You have to trust that too.

At times, the answers to our prayers come directly, almost as if God whispered in our ear, and at other times indirectly, like in the next commercial you see or article you read. You have to pay attention. The answers to your prayers can come in the next song you hear, the next phone call you get, the next person you encounter, etc. Be open to receiving communications from Divine Source in whatever ways they may manifest.

While direct communication works for me, some people like to meditate or do more formal prayers or rituals to connect to their Higher Power. How you choose to connect to your Higher Power is not as important as the effort you put into doing so. It is important to connect to a God of your understanding consistently. Connecting to Source Energy is an exercise in connecting to your Higher Self. The more you practice this strategy, the more likely it will become second nature to do so. You want to make connecting to your Higher Power, that is, connecting to your true self, a habit. The most effective way to speak and live in your authenticity is to be genuinely connected to your true self.

Strategy #2: Mind Your Business

"Mind Your Business"

"Mind your business" is an interesting saying. When you first hear it, you can't help but get defensive. When someone tells me "Mind your business," it's a clear directive that says, "Stay out of my personal matters!" These words may sound harsh, but they set a clear boundary. But I can also understand "Mind your business" to mean I should "Mind *my own* business." In other words, to focus on my personal affairs and stop worrying about what others are doing, thinking, or saying. We all spend too much time and energy focusing on what others are doing, not doing, saying, or not saying, which is an absolute waste of time and energy.

Do you know why we do this? Because it is a lot easier to focus our attention on something external or someone else than it is to focus on ourselves. It's easier to point at someone else and talk about the negative impact of their actions, whether it's the president, your neighbor, your friend, or your family member. It's easy to bad-mouth or blame others because it takes the focus away from ourselves. It is a lot simpler to occupy our time and thoughts by deflecting our attention to someone else's shortcomings than it is to focus on our areas of struggle. However, doing this is not productive and serves no good purpose. Pointing fingers or externalizing blame makes things worse and robs you of the opportunity to learn something new about yourself. It impedes an opportunity for self-growth.

I first became aware of the power and the pretense of focusing externally when I watched the movie Scarface at 13. In this movie, Al Pacino plays a drug dealer named Tony Montana. In one scene, as his character unravels, he has a meltdown in a restaurant and creates an uncomfortable scene for everyone. His character engages in a diatribe that is priceless in my eyes. In a rageful drug-induced state that gave him the bravado to speak his truth freely, he yells at the entire restaurant, "What you lookin' at? You all a bunch of fuckin' assholes. You know why? You don't have the guts to be what you wanna be!? You need people like me. You need people like me so you can point your fuckin' fingers and say, 'That's the bad guy.' So what that make you? Good? You not good. You just know how to hide, how to lie. Me, I don't have that problem. Me, I always tell the truth. Even when I lie. So, say goodnight to the bad guy!" In a moment of rage and clarity, Tony Montana tells everyone that it's much easier to point fingers at the bad guy than to look at our own shortcomings.

We all want a bad guy to point at and blame, so we can feel better about ourselves. Ain't that the truth! Pacino's character points out the lack of genuine self-reflection and honesty in most people and how we focus on the "bad guy" to take attention away from our areas of struggle and flaws. We often prefer to focus on others' negativity as a means of avoiding our areas of conflict or deficits! It's a lot easier to mind other people's business than it is to mind our own! I was an adolescent when I first saw this movie, but even then, the impact of his words was piercing and profound to me!

Focus On You

The allure of focusing on others' actions and behaviors is that it takes away the pressure and responsibility of focusing on ourselves and doing our work. Sadly, most people resist engaging in the meaningful self-care and self-growth processes that will enrich the quality of their lives. I get it, though. The level of work that I am talking about here is challenging and can be exhausting and overwhelming. It's hard to look at our stuff, to look at the role we play in our conflicts and struggles. It's much easier to focus on the external world and blame others. But as long as we keep the focus on others, we'll remain stuck and unable to grow, make changes, or evolve in any meaningful manner.

The hardest work we will ever have to do is to mind our business! Fortunately, it will also be the most gratifying work we ever do. We all need to stop wasting our time and energy focusing on others. Redirect that energy and use it to develop yourself to be the best possible version of you! Most of us focus on tearing others down (judging, gossiping), when we should be focusing on building each other up. But we can't genuinely build anyone else up until we build ourselves up first. Moving forward, mind your business! Focus your time and energy on developing yourself in all areas of your life and see how that works out for you. Our journey towards self-growth will never be easy. However, being honest with ourselves and purposely working to improve our areas of conflict and deficit are critical components of speaking our truth and living life from a space of authenticity.

Do You, Be Intentional

Now that we understand that focusing on others is nothing but a distraction and avoidance of doing our personal growth work, let's look at some core ways to keep our focus on ourselves and naturally evolve into the best possible versions of ourselves.

I MEAN EXACTLY THAT when I say do your work and be the best version of you possible. To be the best you possible, you have to be honest and intentional in all you do. You have to be candid with yourself and with others, and you have to define who you want to be in every moment of every day. Through our actions, we get to decide and declare who we are moment to moment. If you want to be kind, then do something kind for another person. If you want to be compassionate, try to understand what others are going through or why they behave as they do.

To be the best you possible, you cannot let others' actions dictate who you choose to be in a moment. Reacting or being impulsive is disempowering and not a good way to live from your higher self. Think before you act or respond to others or a situation. Decide what character traits you want to embrace at the moment and then consciously choose to embody those traits. To do this, we have to exercise self-control and self-restraint. To live intentionally, we have to be mature and rise above pettiness and behaviors that don't align with who we are choosing to be in a given moment.

Learning to live intentionally takes a lot of patience and practice. First, you have to get to know yourself well. You have to learn what you like and don't like, what you can live with, and what's a deal-breaker. A constant personal inventory takes place as you move in the direction of connecting to your core self and living life from a space of authenticity. As you become accustomed to living life from this point of being, you learn to reinforce and validate your self-growth by behaving in ways that align with the constantly-evolving, best version of you. This process is a key part of personal development. All talk and no action is a fruitless endeavor. Your external behaviors need to align and support your thoughts, intentions, and who you choose to be.

You need to take deliberate action to self-improve and behave in ways that reinforce your evolving beliefs and desires for yourself. You have to validate your intention by taking action. This focus will ensure that your personal growth and development happen in the real world, not just in your fantasy world.

Set Boundaries

Being intentional in our actions provides us the opportunity to create a state of being that honors our integrity and our authenticity. To maintain this way of being, you will have to learn to set clear boundaries with others. As we change and evolve, others are likely going to challenge and test us. People get used to us being a certain way, and they expect us always to be that way. They often want to keep us in a box, if you will, that resonates with who they think we are or who they need us to be, or even who we may have been, not with who we now choose to be. By keeping us in a box, people think they can predict and control our behavior. When we start to change, a lot of resistance often surfaces from the people we interact with because somehow our change doesn't serve them or their agenda, or they do not trust that our change is for the better or even genuine. When this resistance to our change arises, we will need to set clear boundaries that establish limits and set expectations. Put simply, we have to make crystal clear to people the treatment we expect, and what behaviors are and are not acceptable, and the cost or consequences for violating our boundaries. Individuals tend not to react well to limit settings. When you meet resistance, you should interpret this as a cue that you are doing something right, and doing something to take care of yourself. People will often test your boundaries, and it is up to you to firmly reestablish and protect them. Eventually, people will respect your new limit setting, or they will gradually fade away from your life.

Things and people that are not in alignment with your higher self and purpose need to be removed from your life for you to grow. Let them go! Your higher self and purpose await you on the other side of this resistance.

In a similar vein, it is important that we also set boundaries for ourselves. We need to learn which behaviors serve our best interests and which do not. We need to act with integrity and honor our intentions in all we do. We really can't expect others to respect our boundaries if we don't. We have to lead by example. Others will follow our lead. It's therefore important, as I said earlier, that our actions be in alignment with our intentions. Doing this, like everything else, will get easier over time and with consistent practice. When you get to the place where this becomes second nature to you, and you see the value in honoring the integrity of your being, you will inevitably ask yourself why you didn't do this sooner.

Strategy #3: Follow Your Inner Knowing

Our Beliefs

By now, it should be abundantly clear that speaking and living one's truth is easier said than done. The strategies I am outlining are intended to build on one another and give you specific ways to develop the ability to connect to your true self. The more you connect to your core being, the better you become at speaking and living your truth. The more you understand yourself, the better you become at helping others understand you as well.

I cannot emphasize enough the value of connecting to your inner self and the importance of making consistent efforts to remain connected to your true self. Some may assume that this process is automatic, but the truth is that it is not. We are taught from the very beginning of our lives what to believe and how to behave.

Initially, what we believe is made up primarily of what our families taught us. As we grow up, we gradually develop our own belief system. It incorporates a combination of our family's perceptions, our peers' views, and some elements of our society's beliefs and expectations. At some point, what we believe, how we think, and behave becomes a complex smorgasbord (a little of this, a little of that) based on all of our experiences. To keep growing and evolving, it serves us to continuously question and refine our belief system based on recent and actual experiences.

Listen To Your Inner Knowing, Your Intuition, Your Gut

In order to feel like autonomous and individualized beings, we must develop our own set of beliefs based on our actual lived experiences, not based on what our parents, friends, or society believe. An effective way to do this is to attune to and listen to your inner knowing. We all have that little "voice" inside us that is forever chirping away, telling us to do or not do something. Our inner voice is not there to annoy us, make us anxious, or stir up trouble; its purpose is deeper than that. I believe our inner voice is how God communicates directly with each of us. Some people hear it as a whisper in their ear, some feel it in the

51

pit of their stomach, others get goosebumps. Some call this inner knowing a gut feeling, and others call it their intuition. Whatever you call it and however this inner knowing expresses itself to you, make it a habit of paying attention to it and follow its guidance. It's like having a personal internal GPS. When you follow your inner GPS, it keeps you safe and leads you on the best path for you. When you don't follow your internal GPS, you inevitably go in counterintuitive directions and go down paths that take you away from your true self, which is never a good thing. More often than not, this results in a negative experience in which things go haywire, and you will undoubtedly say to yourself, "I knew it. I should have followed my gut."

This inner knowing, your intuition, is The Divine's gift to us all. We are all born and familiar with it. Some call it our sixth sense. The challenge for many of us is in knowing how to identify and trust our inner knowing. Once we can do this, we must learn to allow it to guide us in our daily lives, and our overall growth and development. Trusting our inner knowing is a skill that we develop over time and, like anything else, the more we practice, the better we get at it. You need to start familiarizing yourself with how your intuition communicates with you. Do you get butterflies in your stomach? Do you get goosebumps? Do you hear a whisper? Once you recognize how your gut feeling expresses itself, you have to start connecting consistently to this inner knowing and let it guide you in all things you do.

My Process

I connect to my intuition in a very basic manner. I feel it in the pit of my stomach. For example, when someone asks me to do something or I meet someone for the first time, if I get an instant knot in the pit of my stomach that I cannot explain, that is my cue that something is off, something is not correct. The feeling tells me that I need to proceed with caution. It's almost like my internal alarm has gone off, alerting me to some potential danger. If I disregard this internal alarm system, some drama or conflict inevitably ensues, and I always regret not following my gut feeling.

Let me give you an example of when I failed to follow my inner guidance. One day, early in my relationship with my former spouse, we were arguing while driving in Manhattan. As with all of our arguments, things got intense fast. He was driving, and in a moment of acute rage and frustration, he impulsively *jumped out of his car* and abandoned me and the car in the middle of Manhattan traffic. I was in shock. Who does that? I could not wrap my head around his irrational behavior, and my inner knowing was screaming, "Pay attention! This behavior is madness! Get out of this relationship!" But I didn't listen to my gut. Instead, I simply got in the driver's seat and drove back home. (What I wanted to do was leave his car in the middle of Manhattan, just as he had done. I, however, being a mature adult, did not act on my impulsive desire.) As I drove home, I was acutely aware that he was volatile, erratic, and unstable. I also knew that I should walk away from the dysfunction labeled "Us."

Unfortunately, despite its blaring alarm system, I failed to listen to my inner knowing, and I remained in this chaotic relationship that eventually devolved and caused an immeasurable degree of hurt and loss for many people. This is one of the earliest memories I have of not listening to and following my inner knowing. This recollection is a constant reminder of what can happen when I don't listen to my gut.

Intuition also works for me in positive ways. For example, suppose I experience goosebumps or feel a wave of positive energy and emotions when I'm processing something with someone (like in a therapy session) or when I first meet someone. In that case, that lets me know that I'm on the right path, that whatever we're discussing is on target or that the person I just met is important for me. This is what happened when I first met my best friend, Margarita (I call her Margie; she hates it). The very first day I met her, it was like magic. We hit it off instantly, which is unusual for me since I can be socially awkward with strangers. Within minutes of meeting, we were laughing and joking as if we had known each other forever. My gut instantly liked her, and so did I. That was 20 years ago. Our instant connection evolved into a long-term friendship.

Over the years, I have worked hard to develop this connection to my inner knowing. I consider my intuition to be my direct line to the Creator, God, the Universe, Source Energy, and whatever you call your Higher Power. I believe that our inner knowing is how The Divine communicates with each of us and guides us. This is why it is so important to connect to a God of your understanding; it's how we fully connect to our true selves.

How To Follow Your Intuition

I am a firm believer that we all have the ability to connect with and "speak" directly to our Higher Power and that we can ask for guidance at all times. However, we have to work on our "listening" skills, as the guidance or answers we're seeking can come in a variety of forms. As I said earlier in this book, when I spoke of connecting to a God of your understanding, when you ask for guidance, clarity or understanding, you have to be open to receiving answers in whatever manner they arrive. Our inner knowing, The Divine, communicates in many ways. We have to "see" or "hear" or "feel" the guidance we are seeking when it presents itself.

Another way to connect to your inner knowing is to pray for clarity. I said this earlier as well. By praying, I simply mean to have a conversation with God. Talk to God from your inner heart as if you were talking to your mom or to your best friend. Ask for clear and specific guidance on how to manage whatever situation is presenting itself and have faith that the answer will make itself readily clear to you when the time is right. Whenever I am struggling with a major issue, when I go to sleep, I pray for specific instructions on how to manage whatever is going on. For the most part, my experience has been that the minute I awake, the first thought I have usually spells out how I should proceed. When I receive this type of guidance I honor my intuition, and thus I honor myself, by doing exactly what my inner knowing has instructed me to do.

Our inner knowing, our connection to The Divine in us, will keep us on the path towards expressing our true selves and living life in an authentic manner moment to moment. When we don't utilize this basic, yet extremely valuable tool, we lose a critical component of our being that is intended to help us in our walk, in our truth, and in our purpose. I suggest you become one with this aspect of your being and see how life transforms for you!

If It Feels Right, Do It. If It Doesn't Feel Right, Don't Do It.

When I first thought about the strategy "follow your inner knowing," I considered using the word "good" instead of "right" in the above heading. It would have read, "If it feels good, do it. If it doesn't feel good, don't do it." However, I realized that there are a lot of things that we have to do or need to do that don't necessarily feel good, like eating well or exercising, but we do them anyway because it is in our best interest to do so. Then other things don't feel good, but we should do anyway because they help us grow, stretch, and evolve as human beings. The experiences that push us to grow emotionally, psychologically, and spiritually move us out of our comfort zones. When we are in unfamiliar territory, we become uncomfortable, and that discomfort is what challenges us to expand, grow, and learn something different. Although these moments generally do not feel good, they are necessary for our overall growth and evolution as individuals. Though often hard to embrace, these moments are opportunities to expand and grow. If we avoid these moments because they don't "feel good," we will never do the necessary work to live up to our potential; we will stagnate and continue to repeat our mistakes. Some things feel good at the moment that we should not do or overindulge in, like excessively eating junk food, or drinking alcohol, or engaging in self-serving or destructive behaviors.

To develop your ability to follow your intuition, you have to become keenly aware of how you feel about things and why you feel as you do. You need to have a continuous internal dialogue and check-in with yourself. Ask yourself questions to help you understand your feelings and reactions. This will help you become more self-aware. It will also help you make decisions and act in ways that align with your true self. You have to move away from reacting to things because of whether they feel good or not, and move in the direction of responding to things based on whether they feel right for you or not. To truly follow your inner knowing, you have to do only what intrinsically feels right.

Going against your intuition and what is right for you is never a good idea, no matter how big or small the situation. Being disingenuous to yourself does not serve you or anyone else. It is supremely important for you always to do what is in your best interest, as long as it isn't harmful to others. Do what feels right to you regardless of what others think, say, or believe. It's time to stop people-pleasing. Start honoring your true self and maintain your integrity to self in all you do. This will help you to move consistently in the direction of speaking and living your truth. If you don't take care of yourself and honor your truth first and foremost, who will?

Strategy #4: Speak Your Truth (Especially When Your Voice Shakes)

Masks: Our False Selves

Given that this book is all about speaking your truth, you would think that I would put this next strategy at the frontline, or that I would have detailed how to do so much earlier, but I couldn't. Speaking one's truth is a skill that we need to develop, and we cannot effectively do it until we know how to connect to our core selves. The first three strategies I outlined are intended to help you identify with and relate to your true self. We are all guarded human beings and develop many masks, ways of being that help us navigate the complexities of the world we live in and the people in our lives. Sadly, the masks we develop to manage or survive in our day-to-day lives sometimes become these false selves that take on lives of their own and gradually distance us from our true selves.

We all wear masks. We all play multiple roles (sibling, spouse, friend, boss, etc.) in our lives that require us to be somewhat different. This is normal. I am referring to the experience of acquiescing to these roles, to these false selves, to being defined by external roles that box us into certain ways of being and behaving because it is expected of us, not because it resonates with our core selves. Accepting and taking on, to some degree, some aspects of predetermined roles in our lives is normal. However, when we live our lives based mostly on what others want or expect us to be, do, or become, this distances us from our true selves. At this point, we feel lost or disconnected from the things we do, and the lives we are living start to lose meaning.

We have all experienced this at some point in our lives. We have all had moments when we realize that we are not our genuine selves. When moments such as these start to add up, and we become sufficiently uncomfortable (which can look like depression, anxiety, self-destructive behaviors, etc.), we should undertake a personal inventory. We should refocus on ourselves, reflect on our lack of authenticity, and then intentionally move toward thinking and behaving in ways that align with our true selves. This is when the real work begins. When we feel significantly disconnected from our true selves, we need to ask the hard questions regarding who we are and what defines us. This internal process puts us on the path of connecting to our true selves and understanding our truth. You cannot speak your truth until you know what it is!

Speak Your Soul Truth; It's Worth the Risk

Speaking one's truth is probably the most difficult strategy to practice. It's hard because most of us are not confrontational people by nature. Quite often, speaking our truth, speaking up for ourselves, or what we believe in means we have to take a stand. Sometimes, we have to stand against the majority, and it's hard to stand alone. In these moments, you have to be brave, speak your Soul Truth, and remember that you are never truly alone. Your Higher Power is always with you.

Most of us want to be a part of something, and the risk of speaking our truth and fighting for what we believe in is often too great or too scary because we don't want to feel alienated or be attacked. Making the conscious decision in these moments to speak your truth and stand up for what you believe in is where real change and growth takes place. This is where you truly evolve and take ownership of who you are.

We take a huge risk when we choose to speak our truth. It is not easy. We have to push through our anxiety and fear. Speaking our truth often makes us feel vulnerable and exposed. When we show our softness, our weaknesses, our differences, our individuality, we are vulnerable to being hurt because we have no idea how it will be received. Our willingness to push through our fears, have tough conversations, or take on an opposing or alternative position from the majority pushes us to define who we are. This is where we declare to ourselves, to the world, to the Universe, who we truly are. This is where we speak our Soul Truth.

Be Brave, Especially When Your Voice Shakes

We all have moments that place us in positions where we have to stand up and speak our truth or acquiesce. These moments can occur on a large scale, or appear as small, seemingly insignificant moments. For me, the challenges and the call to speak and live my truth were primarily experienced through bullying. I was bullied most of my entire life. My brothers bullied me by scaring me and making me do things I didn't want to do. My mom bullied me by always using fear tactics to get me to do what she wanted. The kids in my neighborhood tried to bully me. They judged me, alienated me, and stared me down. My classmates tried to bully me by talking about me and trying to start dumb fights. As a result of these experiences, I carried around a lot of internalized anger, anxiety, and fear. At some point, I developed some false bravado as a defense. I created a mask that made me look and act as if I wasn't scared. I pretended to be as tough as all the people around me. But the truth was I was still afraid inside. I had just learned to "fake the funk."

When I became a psychologist, the site of my first job was rough. The organization's culture was riddled with anger, hostility, and antagonism. Everyone was subjected to this dynamic irrespective of their title. I was the new kid on the block. I was young, and I felt unsure of myself in my recently acquired doctor title. I tried to blend in and mind my own business. Unfortunately, I had a co-worker who made it clear that she did not like me for whatever reason. She would be either dismissive or passive-aggressive towards me. Needless to say, I felt challenged and vulnerable, and all my anxiety and fear about bullies in my past resurfaced. It was hard for me to accept that I felt intimidated and scared. I mean, for God's sake, I was a grown woman! How could I possibly feel the same way I did as a child? But I did.

To be a mature adult and manage this experience, I tried to befriend this woman, but she would not have it. The few times I tried to be friendly or cordial, she responded with some form of hostility or negativity. My internal reactions were crazy! I went from being mad to being sad, feeling hurt, being scared, and feeling rejected. I thought, "Why doesn't she like me?" The anxiety I felt every time I had to see her or interact with her was overwhelming, but there was no way to avoid her. I hated how I allowed her to make me feel. I hated even more that, like a classic bully, she could see through my mask and pinpoint my weakness. In this case, the weakness was probably me wanting to be liked by everybody or perhaps me being disingenuous. Whatever she saw, she didn't like it, and neither did I. I struggled with the negative feelings and how I was experiencing myself, namely, like a punk and a fraud.

I am not entirely sure why this woman disliked me, but my best guess is that it was because I was young, intelligent, pretty, a doctor, and I got a lot of attention. She was older, a clerk, and not too friendly. For whatever reason, she was jealous of me and discharged her insecurity directly at me. Eventually, this situation came to a head. I realized I wasn't standing up for myself or speaking my truth. The day came where I had had enough of her nonsense and my own. I realized that although I felt scared and intimidated, it felt far worse not to stand up for myself and speak my truth. I decided to confront her. As I approached her, I tried to control the trembling, the shakiness in my voice, and I tried to drown out the loud sound of my beating heart in my ears as I finally stood up to her! I said firmly, "I know you don't like me, and I don't like you, but we are going to respect one another." As we made eye contact in that poignant moment, a clear, nonverbal exchange took place between us. The message was, "Enough already; let's stop this nonsense." I stood up to the bully. I stood up for what I believed in and for my self-respect. I had spoken my truth and drawn the boundary line. And just like that, the situation resolved itself. Moving forward, there were no more negative exchanges of any kind between us. The animosity dissipated, and we went our separate ways. I had established a clear understanding between us. I set a boundary.

Though this situation was not a big deal, the takeaway for me was huge. It was one of those moments where I challenged and pushed myself to do something that made me uncomfortable! I had to push through my stress and fear and speak up for what I believed in, in a professional and very public setting. That took me out of my comfort zone. By speaking my truth in a moment when I felt intimidated and scared, I validated myself and honored my inner knowing, which had been screaming, "This isn't right! Do something!" I can't even begin to tell you how empowering it was to do something finally.

Speaking and living your truth are what life is about. Doing so when you're scared or intimidated is brave. When you act from a space of bravery, even if your voice shakes, you win because you've grown and expanded your sense of self. You win because you have pushed past a prior limitation. It is essential to give your inner voice an outlet and remain present to the reality that your truth is dynamic, ever-changing, and speaks only to your experience at the moment. Remember that just like you need to speak your truth, others need to voice their truths. We must always make an effort to be mindful of respecting and taking in others' perceptions of truth while still honoring our own.

Strategy #5: Live Your Life, Live Your Truth (No Matter What Everyone Else Thinks, Says, Or Believes)

Little Minions vs. Individual Beings

From the day we are born, we are basically reared to be little minions, robots. We are taught to do whatever our parents, elders, leaders, etc., tell us to do. Our parents and society constantly tell us how to act and what is socially appropriate. On one level, this is necessary. It is important to conform to social expectations and norms otherwise, things would be chaotic. We all need to follow a general template that guides us on being civilized human beings. It's important to respect the law, observe social etiquette, and develop an internal moral compass.

The inherent problem with this process is that we get pushed into being like everyone else in following the status quo. Though we are all the same at a very basic level, we are also all incredibly unique individuals who genuinely desire to express our individuality. (I express mine!) It's quite easy to see this in young children. They freely speak and live their truths. Children have no filters and therefore openly voice their thoughts and feelings. That is a beautiful quality that we should all emulate to some degree. But children can also at times be vicious and mean unintentionally. As responsible adults and guides, we have to temper children's innate desire to candidly speak their truths by teaching them that their words and actions can sometimes be hurtful. We have to teach our children to be honest, while also being kind and compassionate towards others. It is essential that we show our children right from wrong and teach them to be socially appropriate.

The problem for children arises when adults begin to squash and devalue a child's true uniqueness and sense of self. Too often, we tell them that their spontaneity, creativity, and natural essence are unacceptable or inappropriate. When rearing our children, we need to find a balance between rearing socially appropriate, civilized members of society, and creative souls who can express their uniqueness in meaningful ways. This is not an easy thing to do. Instead, this is a complex process that requires parents and society to "see" and honor the individuality of each child. It requires parents to work consciously when teaching their children to express and live their truths in creative ways that honor their essences, while still being civilized and kind. Raising little minions is much easier than raising individual beings who can think for themselves and live in their essences. Teaching children to be honest with others and with themselves in a kind manner is probably one of the most important things a parent can teach a child.

The Power and Value of Honesty for Me

Throughout my early youth, my mother was often dishonest with me. Given all the chaos in our home, my mom was often in tears or acutely anxious. Whenever I asked her what was wrong or what was happening, she would say, "Nothing. Everything is fine." Her dishonesty was maddening as I could see that something was amiss. I am sure that she didn't tell me a lot of things in some warped effort to protect me, but her lack of honesty, more often than not, resulted in me having to sit alone with my fears and worries.

Deceit can be very unsettling for a child. It drove me nuts. In my naiveness, I did not understand the untruths I was told that were intended to protect me, or the inherent value of being socially appropriate, or conforming to the norm. I remember often thinking that Mami was a big, fat liar and that I couldn't trust her. If I could not trust Mami, then I could not trust anyone else. Experiencing so much dishonesty in my early youth was confusing. It made me anxious and angry. The internal angst I often felt led me to rely on my own experiences, what I saw and felt (my gut), to figure out what was occurring in my life and world. At some point in my adolescence, I decided not to be like the dishonest adults in my life. I preferred honesty, so I decided to be candid and to speak my truth. The conscious decision to speak my truth became the first way in which I expressed living my truth.

Unfortunately, deciding to openly voice what I was seeing, feeling, witnessing, or experiencing became the source of much strife in my family, then and now. In my family, I have always pushed for us to evolve in how we communicate and act towards one another - to have tough conversations that push us beyond our comfort zones; conversations in which we challenge one another to be better, own mistakes, and change what gets in the way of overall growth, and our evolution as individuals, and as a family. My way of being has always ignited conflict and resistance (perhaps because we are all on different spiritual and conscious evolutionary levels). But I stand by my integrity to myself and my truth as I continue to evolve. I stand by my position to guide others towards living similarly. I refuse to avoid the tough conversations and confrontations and live in a disingenuous manner. I'm always going to rock the boat and speak my truth, even if it means that I wind up all alone in the boat. I'd rather be alone and live in truth than be surrounded by people who are afraid to jump into the boat with me!

Candor is a key component of living in our truth. One cannot live in integrity if one is not being honest. To live our truth, we must strive to be candid with ourselves and with others at all times. This is easier said than done, and it will require unending practice. To evolve, we must make diligent efforts to speak our truth genuinely; it is a prerequisite to living in our truth.

Life Is a Game, Figure Out Your Game

I have repeatedly stated that I see life as a game, and I invite you to do the same. Adults tend to take life too seriously and using this metaphor can perhaps lighten things up. In thinking about your life as a game, you must first decide what you want this game to look like. For example, do you want to be the Game Master? If so, ask yourself what running the game entails and put in the work to make this happen. The beauty in being the Game Master is that you're always in charge. You get to set the rules. You get to decide who plays with you and who cannot. You get to decide what the end goal is and what winning looks like. Can you even imagine living your life in such an empowered manner? The key to effectively utilizing this metaphor is to figure out the game you want to play and consistently put in the effort to play it to the best of your ability. I chose to play the game of being the best student possible for a long time, and it worked well for me. However, when I was no longer a student, I had to devise a new game to play. Things change in life, and you have to go with the flow. Don't get stuck. Keep growing. Move forward. Stretch and become more significant than you ever imagined possible.

In general, when we think of playing a game, we think of having fun. It's the same with life. It's important to have fun in life. When I speak about living your truth, I'm suggesting that you be both honest and lighthearted in this process. I'm suggesting that you have fun expressing and defining yourself and your truth. Use your imagination and your creativity to explore, discover and express your true self. Be patient and give yourself plenty of opportunities to recreate and revise the best version of YOU as your clarity and self-awareness increase. Remember that we are dynamic beings that are forever changing and evolving. How you live and express your truth will change as you do. Don't worry about what others think, say, or believe. Keep the focus on you.

When I say "play your game," I mean live the life that you want to live, regardless of others' opinions. Life is short. Have fun! Time and experience have taught me that having fun and enjoying yourself is how you win the game of life. Think of it like this: if you're playing your game attuned to your true self, you should be enjoying it! If you're not having fun, pay attention to this. Perhaps the Universe is telling you that something isn't right, that something has to change. If this is so, then figure out what has to change and adjust it. Do whatever is necessary to secure the change that will put you back in alignment with your true self. Take action! You have all the power and all the control when you play YOUR game and not theirs. You should always aim to live life from an empowered position and constructively do whatever you have to do to put yourself in the position to play your game and win.

Allow Yourself to Be Vulnerable, Take the Risk

Allowing yourself to be vulnerable is an important part of living your truth. Let's define vulnerability—the word vulnerable means to be susceptible to physical or emotional harm. The idea of getting hurt in any way is scary, and so we generally avoid it at all costs. This makes logical sense. We all have some degree of literal or metaphorical armor that defends and protects us from getting hurt. We would be foolish not to have some form of protection to keep us safe at all times. Life's challenges and experiences teach us that we need to safeguard ourselves against real and perceived threats. The idea or the suggestion that we should allow ourselves to be vulnerable seems counterintuitive. Why would anyone knowingly place themselves in a position where they could get hurt? The answer is simple: taking risks and opening yourself up to live life from a space of vulnerability is where life gets rich. It's where real intimacy is created, where we honor our true selves, where self-growth occurs.

Being brave enough to walk in your truth even when you are afraid, and taking risks that push you out of your comfort zone and leave you vulnerable are not easy tasks. Living in your truth and taking risks are incredibly challenging together and might occasionally place you in a position where you feel alone, attacked, or invalidated. Being vulnerable is probably the hardest thing to do. It can make us feel soft, weak, exposed, or outright unsafe on every level. However, in being vulnerable, we truly allow ourselves to see, show, and live our truth and connect to others in meaningful ways. When we are brave enough to let others see our imperfections and our vulnerabilities, we are liberated from hiding behind masks we tend to wear. In these candid moments, we genuinely connect to others because we allow them to see authentic aspects of ourselves that we generally don't freely display.

Vulnerability means exposing your thoughts and feelings to others. In openly sharing our experiences, we sometimes learn that our perception is skewed or that perhaps things are not as they appear to be. In other words, when we're vulnerable, we sometimes discover that our beliefs and our truths are incorrect or based on misperceptions. No one ever wants to be wrong. No one likes being called out for the role they may have played in a situation. However, listening is an important component of being vulnerable. Hearing what others have to say or how others perceive things is a crucial aspect of being vulnerable. Engaging in this co-creative process is where the real healing work takes place. When we allow ourselves to be vulnerable and speak our truth, we give others the same opportunity. This is how we work through the conflicts and barriers that impede the development of genuine, safe, and intimate communication and relationships.

Being vulnerable is about taking big risks; it's about the things that scare you and push you to grow. Sometimes the risk-taking is in speaking your truth. Other times, the risk is in living your truth and doing the BIG THINGS that push you to be greater, going for things that are challenging. It's applying for that job you know you can do, but don't think you'll get, or writing that bestseller that you have inside of you but are afraid to put out there. Living your truth is walking in your light and greatness, honoring who God intended you to be, and fulfilling your purpose. All of these things and more are what being vulnerable and taking risks look like. What does being vulnerable look like for you?

Sadly, fear of being hurt, rejected, or ridiculed often stops us from being vulnerable and taking the risks that make life worth living. People don't allow themselves to be vulnerable in this way because in moving out of our comfort zones, we take chances at being told "No." We risk rejection or failure. No one wants to fail or be rejected. It's easier to play it safe, not open yourself up to vulnerability. However, playing it safe stops your growth and marginalizes you. We are all meant to be great and do amazing things. Playing small does not serve anyone well. Be the awesome you that you were born to be! Take the risk, enjoy the challenge, and embrace the opportunity. Be open to change and a world of possibilities that will help you grow and serve in the way that only you can. You will never know what is possible for you unless you try. The worst thing that can happen is that you learn something new about yourself or life. Sometimes learning the lesson is what taking the risk was all about. Being vulnerable is where this game called Life gets rich. Either way, you have to trust the process. When you live in your truth, you always win!!!

Strategy #6: Have an Attitude of Gratitude

Focus On the Good That Is Present

Finally, I cannot emphasize enough the simplicity and importance of being grateful for what you have, for what is present in your life and your experiences. So many of us focus on what we do not have, what we lack, which does not feel good on any level. We should be focusing on all the good things that are present in our lives, be it health, family, home, love, etc. We need to consciously CHOOSE to be grateful for what we have and see how that will attract more things to be thankful for.

This strategy is all about DECIDING what your mindset is going to be. Put another way, it's choosing what kind of filter you want to process the world through. It's like deciding between being an optimist or a pessimist. Which feels better? Which serves you better? I know I am oversimplifying it, that this is much easier said than done. The challenge for many of us is that sadly, we're often exposed to unending negativity in our lives, beginning in early youth, by our loved ones, peers, the media, our community, etc. Many of us are reared to be jaded or distrusting, to look for the bad, and expect the worst. People often believe that focusing on the negative is self-protective and necessary for our survival and well-being. The unfortunate reality is that the world can be a cruel, ugly, and scary place. However, it is also true that the world can be kind, loving, and filled with joy and things that feel good!

When we are young, vulnerable, and impressionable, we have very little conscious choice regarding how we perceive our world and the people in it. As children, we model how our parents or caretakers view the world. Whatever perspective they embrace is likely to be the one we embrace as well. But as we develop and mature, we get to choose whether to keep following our caregiver's model or develop our own. If our parent's perception of the world was primarily optimistic, we should embrace this positive frame and develop it further. But if their view of the world was pessimistic and overly negative, it may not serve us to hold on to this perspective. It's a self-fulfilling prophecy: what you believe in will ultimately manifest itself in your life. If you truly expect and believe in the positive outcome of things, that is what you will experience.

Choose To Be Positive

One of the powers that we have as adults is that we get to make informed decisions. Unlike children, we have the cognitive abilities to think about things and make decisions based on our best interests. Choosing to be positive and to have an attitude of gratitude is probably one of the most important decisions we can make. Having an attitude of gratitude is a great tool for developing or maintaining a positive mind frame. Having an attitude of gratitude does not mean that you ignore reality. If things are horrible, that is your truth. You can't lie to yourself. I suggest that you make a deliberate effort to choose to see some goodness in all situations. What I am suggesting is that you intentionally choose to look for the positive elements in everything. This takes work and can be overwhelming when the problems or circumstances you face are very hard or scary. However, the potential benefit of choosing to look for the good in all situations is invaluable.

How I Search for The Good in A Bad Situation

I have shared that Mami was always afraid and worried. I knew that life was rough for mom growing up. I understood why she was jaded. She always expected the worst and was paranoid by nature. As I grew up, observed, and took her in, I naturally modeled my outlook after hers. Whenever something went wrong, my reaction was fatalistic. Like my mom, I, too, became overly fearful and anxious. To this day, worried and afraid are my baseline. There is no denying it. My initial reaction to any challenge is usually one of anxiety, fear, or pessimism. It's almost like I feel compelled to let these fears and negative feelings wash over me like a tidal wave. This is my modus operandi. I truly cannot help reacting this way. However, once the wave crashes, so to speak, I start to look for the potentially positive elements in the situation. How quickly I recover from the crashing wave depends on the situation that presents itself. Some waves are easier to overcome than others. For me, every time a tidal wave hits, internally, I hold on for dear life to the life preserver I visualize. Then, as the initial wave of panic subsides, and I realize I haven't died, I start to look for the opportunity to present itself in the current situation that will allow me to expand and grow. The harsher the wave, the more challenging the experience, the greater the opportunity for personal growth. The tidal wave takes me out of my comfort zone. Being in this uncomfortable space presents me with the possibility of experiencing defeat, or the opportunity to stretch and move towards genuine personal growth.

In understanding how I experience and manage things, I have to acknowledge that although I learned my negative baseline from Mami, she also taught me to look for the good in everything. I learned it through observing how she used her faith in God to accept things that happened and her belief that everything happens for a reason, that there is Divine intervention in all occurrences. It's true that Mami's reaction to all challenges and conflicts was first to panic and freak out. At some point, though, she would accept what was happening and then move towards understanding why God presented this experience to her. Though she did not always understand why things occurred, she always accepted God's will and way, and she trusted the process in God's Divine plan for her and her children. My mother's faith in God was unshakeable. As I grew up, I, too, developed a strong faith in God and believe that everything has a reason and a purpose. Even when things are not looking good, I lean in and move towards accepting and trusting the process, knowing that ultimately, everything happens for a reason and things will work themselves out.

Admittedly, it's tough to have an attitude of gratitude when things are falling apart. However, being optimistic and having faith will keep you above water when the waves hit; it'll also help you look for the good in all situations. Having an attitude of gratitude is a choice. Making a conscious decision to focus on and look for the good in things, regardless of life's circumstances, is not an easy process. However, I truly believe that if we choose to see the positive, it is inevitable that we will eventually see it and will then attract more positive outcomes into our lives. It's the law of the Universe, the law of attraction, and a self-fulfilling prophecy.

Avoid Stinkin' Thinkin'

Having an attitude of gratitude requires a lot of work. The key to being grateful is to choose to remain positive and see the good in all things, as I stated above. Avoiding "stinkin' thinkin'" is another way of saying "Stay positive." In thinking about how powerful our thoughts are, I consider it worthwhile to spell out in this section some key ways to manage our negative thoughts, and control the "stinkin' thinkin'" that often makes us miserable or steals our joy.

Let me start by defining "stinkin' thinkin.'" It is the process wherein we entertain our fears and worries, where we let our imaginations run wild and think about all the negative things that are happening, have happened, or can potentially happen. Admittedly, it's hard to avoid thinking negatively. It's almost impossible to avoid some pessimistic thoughts. The problem is not that you have negative thoughts. Instead, the problem is when you choose to stay engaged in thinking negatively. When we let our negative thoughts control us, we are setting ourselves up for conflict. It is often the case that one negative thought leads to another and then another. Before you know it, you're stuck in a web of negativity that is pervasive and feels like quicksand.

As a psychologist, I truly appreciate how difficult it can be to control one's thoughts. Let me provide you with two specific strategies that I use that can help control our negative thoughts. I like to visualize things because it helps make things more real; it can help you see and feel things. For example, imagine that your thoughts are like a train moving along smoothly on its tracks. All of a sudden, a negative thought seeps in. This negative thought has the potential to become a **Runaway Train** with no brakes. If your stinkin' thinkin' continues, this runaway train gradually speeds up, reaching maximum velocity, and then there's no stopping it! Your non-stop negative thoughts have now spiraled out of control, and you're caught in this treacherous funk of nasty, horrible thoughts and feelings. If we don't stop the negative thoughts, the runaway train will keep going! To stop the train and end our pessimistic thought process, there are two options. We can either stay on this runaway train and wait for the inevitable crash (which usually looks like anger, frustration, anxiety, sadness, depression, impulsive acting out, etc.), or we can **make deliberate efforts** to stop the chain of negative thoughts that is fueling this runaway train. To stop this negative spiral, we have to switch the metaphoric train tracks **intentionally**; that is, we have to redirect our negative thoughts to more positive ones. To effectively do this, we must **purposely do something** to shift our attention away from the negativity consuming us at that moment. We have to **make a conscious decision** to think about something that brings us peace and joy, or we have to engage in an activity that will distract us deliberately. Either of these two things will short-circuit the chain of negative thoughts that are fueling the runaway train and will pull you away from the stinkin' thinkin.'

The fascinating thing about these "runaway train" thoughts is that the process can be so subtle at times that we are not even aware that it is happening or happened. Most of us are so accustomed to thinking negatively that we are not even aware when we do it or that we've boarded that stinkin' thinkin' train. For me, negative thinking starts out above ground in conscious thought and then goes underground into unconscious thinking. I'm not even aware that it's happening until I notice that all of a sudden, I'm feeling moody or irritable (inevitably due to the underlying negative thoughts that I'm entertaining). At this point, I become aware that my stinkin' thinkin' has probably spiraled out of control. When I am lucky enough to realize that I'm on a "runaway train," I deliberately do something to stop or switch this unproductive process. Sometimes this is simple, and the awareness alone makes me stop because it usually feels terrible. Other times, I have to literally tell myself out loud, "Just stop!" Still other times, I have to distract myself consciously: play music, call someone, exercise, etc. I have to intentionally do whatever it takes to stop the negative thoughts that have spiraled out of control. Controlling our thoughts is never easy. It is, however, incredibly empowering to be able to learn to do so. Try this strategy out the next time you're engaged in stinkin' thinkin' and see if it works for you.

The other strategy I use to control my negative thinking is to **"Change the Channel."** Let me give you an example. When my youngest niece was about six, she struggled with horrible nightmares and was afraid of monsters. She was so frightened that she worried about going to sleep at night and having more scary dreams, even in the daytime. Her anxiety and fear escalated as her nightmares continued. We felt powerless, sad, and heartbroken as we watched her go through this turmoil as a family. There was very little we could do other than comfort her and reassure her that they were only dreams, that the fear resulted from the overactive imagination that she could control. While all of this was true, it did very little to help her. The adults told this young child to do what most adults struggle to accomplish: control her imagination, and not talk about what is causing her fear. Think only about the good things that make you happy. This is much easier said than done!

One day while my niece was sitting on my lap talking about her scary thoughts and her fears, she told me, "I can't make it stop. I'm scared." It broke my heart to hear her vulnerability. Then I got an idea, like a light bulb turned on. I told her that her thoughts were like different TV channels in her mind and that if she didn't like what she was "watching" (i.e., seeing/feeling/experiencing) on one channel, all she had to do was "change the channel!" Then she asked the magic question, "How do I do that?" I told her that just like the TV remote control in her home, she also has a pretend remote control for her thoughts, and she can change whatever was "playing" in her mind whenever she wanted to. In her youthful innocence, she said, "But at home, Papi controls the remote." I couldn't help but laugh out loud! I then explained to her that while Papi controlled the TV remote control at home, only she could control the "TV" in her mind.

I clarified for her that our minds have all these different "channels" for our thoughts, feelings, likes, dislikes, etc., and that when we tune in to a specific channel, we can only see what is on that channel. I then asked her to put her hands up to the corners of her eyes to show that she could only see what was in front of her. Then I told her that if she didn't like what she was "watching" on that channel, all she had to do was "change the channel" by looking in a different direction, and I then gently shifted her body position several times to demonstrate my point. With every slight shift, she was able to experience how simple it was to change what she saw, what she was focusing on. I explained to this very young child that her thoughts and feelings operated similarly. Whatever she was focusing on in a given moment is exactly what she was going to experience. Though she was quite young and probably didn't fully grasp the depth of what I was saying to her, at that moment, I gave my niece a simple yet powerful tool and taught her that she has the power to control her stinkin' thinkin'! This strategy proved so helpful that even now, whenever my niece or any of us in the family is in a negative space, we tell them to "change the channel!"

Stinkin' thinkin' can be toxic. It makes us miserable. It's like taking negativity and putting it under a magnifying glass; with each passing thought, the stinkin' thinkin' gets bigger and uglier, which causes us to feel worse. I genuinely believe that stinkin' thinkin' is a root cause of most unhappiness. If we learn to control our thoughts, we have the power to control how we experience things. We need to avoid stinkin' thinkin' and intentionally choose to stay positive. No doubt, at first, staying positive will be challenging. However, as with anything else, practice makes perfect. The more you practice focusing on the good things in your life and consciously choosing to be positive, the better you will become at attracting more positive outcomes into your life. Staying positive is a habit that you can develop. It will serve you well always.

Part V – Do the Work- How To Live by The Strategies

The Three P's: Prayer, Presence, Patience (or Practice, Practice, Practice)

I have said repeatedly that my perspective on life is that it is like a game and that you should approach it as you would any game: figure out the rules of the game you're playing, develop key strategies to play effectively, aim to win, and have fun along the way. I have shared some of my experiences to help you better understand how this specific frame evolved for me and the specific strategies I developed to play my game, my way. The intention behind my sharing was to share the importance of living life as authentically as possible and provide some key strategies to help all that read this do the same for themselves.

Though my frame of viewing life as a game may not fully resonate with everyone, the strategies I have outlined can serve as a useful guide to help us all live our lives in manners that make sense to us, feel authentic, and help us stay connected to our true selves. As with any game, though, knowing the rules or developing theoretical strategies is not enough. You have to play the game. You have to be in action. You have to put some work and effort into understanding and mastering the rules, the strategies, and the game that is your life. To do this, I suggest you utilize the Three P's. Some best understand this as "practice, practice, practice," or as I tell my clients: Prayer, Presence, and Patience.

Prayer

Let's start with prayer. I said earlier that prayer is simply having a conversation with the Divine, with a God of your understanding. Prayer requires one to be humble and vulnerable. Prayer is speaking your truth with the Divine Source and asking for guidance in understanding why things unfold as they do. Prayer is asking The Creator of all that is to help you accept that everything happens for a reason. Prayer is asking for help to see how to move through life in a manner that maintains integrity to your core self. I believe in the power of prayer. It's important to pray and ask for guidance and support in your daily life as you try to incorporate the strategies I have outlined into the context of daily living. Using these strategies as a guideline for speaking and living your truth will not be an easy process by any means. But if you commit to it, the results will be invaluable. You can't fail if you stay consistent in your efforts and if you are grateful along the way for each step that you take forward. So, pray for guidance and express your gratitude for all you already have and all you will receive.

Presence

Presence is also important. Remain aware of your overall process. Be mindful of how you feel or where you are emotionally and psychologically. You have to be honest with yourself for this process to work. So many of us lie to ourselves about how we feel or how much effort we devote to something. But you cannot lie to the Almighty Creator. Trust me, as a psychologist, I can assure you that you can't even lie to yourself forever. It's important to be truthful to yourself, first and foremost. Make an effort to be genuine to yourself about your experiences, your beliefs, your thoughts, and your feelings. Your ability to be authentic is contingent upon your ability to look at yourself and your actions as honestly as possible. Please be kind to yourself in doing this, especially when you become aware of aspects of yourself that you do not like. My firstborn niece, when not at her best, would say, "This is not who I am; it's where I'm at." Yes! This cannot be said any better or more precisely. In the moments when we are not walking in our light and greatness, it's imperative to be honest with ourselves. We need to acknowledge when we are not being true to our core selves. Then, we need to make a conscious decision to do better, to be better for ourselves and all the people in our lives. The value of being present cannot be emphasized enough.

Patience

Finally, we have to have patience with ourselves and with others. Remember, Rome was not built in a day. It takes time to build something beautiful and powerful. You have to first build a strong foundation. The evolution of you living in authenticity is a dynamic process that has to grow and flourish at its own pace. It will take you time to figure out your truth and understand what works or doesn't work for you. Be patient as you learn to integrate these strategies into your life and make them a part of your daily living. The more you utilize this guidance system, the better you will become at living in your authenticity, and at speaking and living your truth. This will not be an easy journey. You will need to have patience. You will need to trust the process and remember that you are not alone in this journey. As with anything else that you want to become good at, you will need to practice, practice, practice with Prayer, Presence, and Patience!

As you live your life and make an effort to speak and live your truth, remind yourself of the Three P's (prayer, presence, and patience) when you feel challenged or overwhelmed. Consistently put in the necessary effort to live your truth and see how you will gradually move in the direction of living your best life. Life is a journey; enjoy the process.

Epilogue

Writing this book was a challenging process for me. I wanted it to be inclusive, so everyone who reads it will reap the same benefits from these strategies as I have. At some point, I came to peace with the reality that my particular frame of viewing the world, and the mechanisms I have used to navigate through my own life might not necessarily be helpful to everyone. I will be forever grateful if at least one person finds this book helpful. I am, however, hopeful that my sharing will positively impact many more.

To those who read this transcript to the end and work this process: remember that consistent effort is the key to success. The guidelines I'm offering are not easy to follow and live by. It takes courage and effort to speak and live your truth. You have to be willing to take risks, and you have to be brave enough to take a leap of faith. I hope these strategies serve you as they do me and help you connect to your true self and others in as genuine a manner as possible. More than anything else, my desire for you is that as you learn to connect to your core self, it will become easier to relate to others, and you will be able to break through any barriers that may cause you to feel stuck (i.e., like you've stopped growing) in life.

As you do your work, remember that life is an evolutionary process for us all and that our truth will change as we do. Life experiences will continuously alter our perceptions and mold new versions of truth and us. Be aware of this, and do not fear change. Wherever life takes you and whatever it looks like moving forward, aim to always live in your truth and fulfill your purpose.

Be intentional in all you do.

Be great.

Be you.

May your journey towards your truth be a great one.

About The Author

Juanita P. Guerra is a licensed clinical psychologist in New York. The first fifteen years of her career she worked in a small community based mental health clinic and then a public hospital primarily serving underprivileged individuals in poverty-stricken areas. While her experiences were rich and gratifying, she eventually felt stunted and responded to an inner calling that desired to do more.

In 2009 she followed her intuition and pursued the call to be greater. She established a small private practice and worked as a consultant to social services departments and the court system to service at-risk youth and their families. This work allowed her to see more clearly the struggle individuals and their families experience as they try to navigate the demands of daily living and the imbalances created in their lives by cultural and societal expectations.

Dr. Guerra eventually realized that most people simply desire to be happy and to live their lives in a manner that feels genuine. While this sounds easy enough to achieve, the reality is that from the day we are born, our experience with the world begins to mold us into a compromised version of ourselves that is generally far removed from who we are at our core. This pivotal realization prompted Dr. Guerra to engage clients therapeutically in a manner that goes beyond the expectations of traditional therapy. Dr. Guerra's sole (Soul) focus now is to help clients learn how to connect to their true selves and diminish the unnecessary suffering most people seem to endure as the result of this disconnect from their core Self. Dr. Guerra's therapeutic work has evolved to incorporate her Spiritual mission: to help individuals connect to their genuine selves so that they can live their lives from a space of authenticity, embrace the God given gifts they have, and live in their purpose.

While her desire and passion to serve was great, Dr. Guerra humbly realized the limits of her reach and ability to impact the world. The idea for this book surfaced in the midst of a personal breakdown that pushed her to look at her life and the areas where she lacked authenticity. It is her desire to share her story of suffering, loss, learning, and triumph with the hope that it will help others to grow, to expand, and to engage life in a manner that feels genuine to them.

Dr. Guerra is also a certified mental health panel expert in the New York Courts system, a certified hypnotherapist, a certified breath therapist and she has specialized forensic training in childhood sexual abuse and trauma. Dr. Guerra also has extensive training on developing one's consciousness and leadership abilities. She believes that doing one's self-growth work and living in one's truth is the key to happiness and living life authentically.